The Principles of

State and Government in Islam

Published under the auspices of

THE NEAR EASTERN CENTER

University of California, Los Angeles

The Principles of
State and Government in Islam

MUHAMMAD ASAD

UNIVERSITY OF CALIFORNIA PRESS
Berkeley and Los Angeles · 1961

University of California Press
Berkeley and Los Angeles, California

Library of Congress Catalog Card No.: 61-7539

Printed in The Netherlands
by Mouton & Co · The Hague

Arabic type set
by E. J. Brill · Leiden

FOREWORD

No statement in the field of history and in the social sciences in general, however analytical in intent and however careful in its documentation, can escape an ambiguity inherent in historical cognition as such which will make it at the same time a presentation of facts and a program, and hence a source of intellectual history yet to be written. The facile charge that no historian can divest himself of bias—a charge too often made in order to discredit uncomfortable insights—needs to be replaced by the acknowledgment that an author's aspiration determines his ability to find and especially to utilize facts in a context relevant thereto.

The aspiration may remain hidden or implicit. The political intent of al-Māwārdi's (d. 1058) comprehensive statement on the structure of the Muslim state was brought to light only slightly less than nine hundred years after the author's death, even though we may be certain that his contemporaries were alive not only to the pertinence of Māwārdi's theses to their immediate situation but to the programmatic significance of his analysis of the caliphate. The function of a work of history or political science may vary in different contexts of time, environment, and civilization. To Western readers, Māwārdi's treatise remains primarily a document of Islamic thinking on the role of the state, and in this sense it represents an objective source for the study of a definite approach to the problem of social organization. In its original context, it must have partaken importantly of the character of a manifesto to form or modify that very approach.

Thus, Mr. Asad's statement on *The Principles of State and Government in Islam* has a double significance. Unlike Māwārdi's *Institutes of Rulership (al-Aḥkām as-sulṭāniyya)*, it is frankly presented as a program. This is the moment, Mr. Asad explains, when the Islamic peoples possess the free choice of their destiny; it is now, or perhaps never, that they can become "Islamic polities in the true sense of the word" (p. 1). Motivated by his awareness of the fleeting uniqueness of the hour, Mr. Asad presents his concept of the Islamic state and attempts to formulate a workable constitution in considerable detail, basing his views on the commonly accepted authoritative sources of Islamic reasoning: the Koranic Revelation and the Sunna, or Tradition, of the Prophet Muhammad. However, his is not the only concept of the Islamic state which is now effective, and hence, from another point of view, his program loses its absoluteness and intellectual autonomy to become one of many pieces of evidence symptomatic of conflicting ideological currents within what is somewhat casually called the Muslim world. The double significance that his book thus acquires for us is enhanced by the fact that the views Mr. Asad expounds are those of a large and influential section of the Muslim public.

His ideas are offered as an objectively and universally valid interpretation of the Muslim message; but the public Mr. Asad wishes to influence is an Islamic one—more specifically, the politically self-conscious Muslim circles of Pakistan. His purpose imposes on him a certain methodological procedure and a manner of presentation that has been developed in this milieu which may be somewhat out of the ordinary to the Western reader. His public is less sensitive to anachronism than ours, after some hundred and fifty years of historicism. The use of the revealed text as the sole cogent proof of an argument imposes techniques of selection and interpretation which would have been familiar to Western discussants of science and religion one or two centuries ago, but which now, on occasion, appear unwarrantedly wilful. The occidental reader should bear in mind that the reinterpretation of scriptural and comparable data to corroborate innovating tendencies and original ideas is, in the intellectual framework of the society to which Mr. Asad addresses himself, the only means to reconcile authority with freedom.

Thus, in effect this book has to be read on three levels simultaneously. It is first and foremost a declarative document. It expounds a view of the state which the author conceives of as an absolute—as the fulfillment of demands on man and society which are implicit in the immutable core of Revelation and Tradition. To Western readers, however, it may represent an attempt to harmonize modern Western-inspired political ideas with the heritage of the Muslim tradition. It is, in this sense, not only an expository but also a confessional document and, in due proportion, to be classified with Calvin's *Institutes* or the *Communist Manifesto*.

But it is equally valuable as a document of present Muslim, or, more precisely, Pakistani thinking on an important matter of immediate, practical urgency. In fact, it deserves to be described as an unusually well-organized and well-phrased statement of a viewpoint that, until very recently, may have been dominant among the educated Islam-conscious intelligentsia in the countries of Arabic tongue as well as in Pakistan.

Finally, the work reflects a certain phase of Westernization; that is, of a more or less deliberate *rapprochement* of the two traditions. This *rapprochement* is sought not only in the political aspiration as such, but also in the method by which it is placed before the reader who is to be convinced that the traditional presuppositions lead naturally to modernistic conclusions, and that these conclusions, in turn, represent the culmination of the true intent of the religious message from which the Islamic heritage developed. The *coincidentia traditionum* validates both—or in a phraseology perhaps more acceptable to the conservative believer, it unveils the infinite wealth of the Muslim revelation by the demonstration that the best of the Western heritage is germinally contained therein.

The manuscript was prepared under the sponsorship of the Haji Anisur Rahman Memorial Society of Karachi, Pakistan, and it was the society's initiative that led the Near Eastern Center of the University of California, Los Angeles, to arrange for its publication. The desire of the society to have it appear in the

West bespeaks an understanding of the transcultural significance of the book and the problems with which it deals.

If any conclusion on the editorial policy of the Near Eastern Center may be derived from our undertaking the responsibility for this publication, it is this: We are alive to the manifold functions and roles that scientific thought assumes in varying contexts; and we shall endeavor in future publications to further scholarship by presenting disquisitions as well as documents, while remaining aware that the classification of any given contribution will depend largely on the cultural context in which it is viewed.

G. E. von Grunebaum, Director
Near Eastern Center
University of California, Los Angeles

PREFACE

This book represents a development of ideas first set forth in my essay, *Islamic Constitution-Making*, which was published in English and Urdu under the auspices of the Government of the Panjab in March, 1948.

At that time I was Director of the Department of Islamic Reconstruction, a government institution devoted to the elaboration of the intellectual and sociolegal principles which should underlie our new society and our new state. Among the problems which preoccupied me most intensely was, naturally enough, the question of the future constitution of Pakistan. The shape which that constitution should have was then, as it is now, by no means clear to everybody. Although the people of our country were, for the most part, imbued with enthusiasm for the idea of a truly Islamic state—that is, a state based (in distinction from all other existing political groupments) not on the concepts of nationality and race but solely on the ideology of Qur'ān and Sunnah—they had as yet no concrete vision of the methods of government and of the institutions which would give the state a distinctly Islamic character and would, at the same time, fully correspond to the exigencies of the present age. Some elements of the population naïvely took it for granted that, in order to be genuinely Islamic, the government of Pakistan must be closely modeled on the forms of the early Caliphate, with an almost dictatorial position to be accorded to the head of the state, utter conservatism in all social forms (including a more or less complete seclusion of women), and a patriarchal economy which would dispense with the complicated financial mechanism of the twentieth century and would resolve all the problems of the modern welfare state through the sole instrumentality of the tax known as *zakāt*. Other sectors—more realistic but perhaps less interested in

Islam as a formative element in social life—visualized a development of Pakistan on lines indistinguishable from those commonly accepted as valid and reasonable in the parliamentary democracies of the modern West, with no more than a formal reference in the wording of the constitution to Islam as the "religion of the State" and, possibly, the establishment of a "Ministry of Religious Affairs" as a concession to the emotions of the overwhelming majority of the population.

It was no easy task to construct a bridge between these two extremes. What was needed was the outline of a constitution which would be Islamic in the full sense of the word and would also take the practical requirements of our time into consideration: a demand that was justified by our conviction that the social scheme of Islam supplies valid answers to problems of all times and all stages of human development. Nevertheless, the existing Islamic literature offered no guidance in our difficulty. Some Muslim scholars of earlier centuries—especially of the ʿAbbāsid period—had bequeathed to us a number of works on the political law of Islam; but their approach to the problems had naturally been conditioned by the existing cultural environment and by the sociopolitical requirements of *their* time, and the results of their labors were therefore inapplicable to the needs of an Islamic state in the twentieth century. The available modern Muslim works on the same subject, on the other hand, suffered as a rule from too great a readiness to accept the political concepts, institutions, and governmental methods of modern Europe as the norm to which (in the opinion of these authors) a modern Islamic state should conform: an attitude which in many cases resulted in the adoption by these authors of many concepts which were diametrically opposed to the true demands of Islamic ideology.

Thus, neither the works of our predecessors nor those of our contemporaries could furnish a satisfactory conceptual basis on which the new state of Pakistan should be built up. Only one way remained open to me: to turn to the original sources of Islamic Law—Qurʾān and Sunnah—and to work out on their basis the concrete premises of the future constitution of Pakistan independently of all that has been written on the subject of the Islamic state. In pursuance of this aim—and aided by the many years of study which I had previously devoted to the Qur'ān, the science of *ḥadīth*, or Tradition, and the methodology of *fiqh*, or jurisprudence —I decided to draw the theoretical outline of an Islamic constitution on the strength of the clear-cut political injunctions forthcoming from the Qur'ān and from authentic *aḥādīth*. While the fundamental principles underlying this outline were provided by the Qur'ān, most of the relevant details and the method of their application were gained from about seventy sayings of the Apostle of God bearing on various sociopolitical aspects of the community's life. The result of my endeavors was the above-mentioned lengthy essay on *Islamic Constitution-Making*. Owing to political developments which need not be discussed here, only very few, if any, of my suggestions have been utilized in the (now abolished) Constitution of the Islamic Republic of Pakistan: perhaps only in the Preamble, adopted by the Constituent Assembly in 1949, can an echo of those suggestions be found.

Now, after the unfortunate experiences of the past decade, the problem of Pakistan's constitutional future is still unresolved; and it seems to me, therefore, that a discussion of the principles which ought to underlie the constitution of an Islamic state has not outlived its usefulness. On the contrary, the very fact that none of the existing Muslim countries has so far achieved a form of government that could be termed genuinely Islamic makes a continuation of the discussion imperative—at least to people to whom Islam represents the dominant reality in their lives. The present book is an attempt to keep that discussion alive. Unavoidably, some of my conclusions will give rise to controversy; but I have always believed —and believe now more than ever—that without a stimulating clash of opinions there can be no intellectual progress in Muslim society; and that the Prophet's saying,

إختلاف علماء أمتى رحمة

"The differences of opinion among the learned of my community are a sign of God's grace," has a positive, creative value which has only too often been overlooked in the course of Muslim history—to the detriment of Muslim social progress.

I cannot conclude without expressing my deep gratitude to the Haji Anisur Rahman Memorial Society of Karachi, who have sponsored and encouraged this work and made it possible for me to present it to my fellow-Muslims of Pakistan.

Muhammad Asad

CONTENTS

Chapter I

THE ISSUE BEFORE US

Why an Islamic State?

In the life of every nation there comes, sooner or later, a moment when it seems to be given a free choice of its destiny: a moment when the decisions as to which way to go and what future to aim at, seem to be freed from the pressure of adverse circumstances, and when no power on earth is able to prevent the nation from choosing one way in preference to another. Such historic moments are extremely rare and fleeting, and it may well be that if a nation fails to avail itself of the opportunity thus offered, it will not be offered another for centuries to come.

This moment of free choice has now arrived for the nations of the Muslim world. After a century of struggles, hopes, errors, and disappointments, full independence from colonial rule has been won by most of the countries inhabited by Muslims. The achievement of independence has brought to the foreground the question of the fundamental principles by which they should govern themselves in order to ensure happiness and well-being for their peoples. The problem is one not merely of administrative efficiency but also of ideology. It is for the Muslims to decide whether their newly independent states shall be subordinated to modern Western concepts which deny to religion the right to shape the nation's practical life, or shall, at last, become Islamic polities in the true sense of the word. A state inhabited predominantly or even entirely by Muslims is not necessarily synonymous with an "Islamic state": it can become truly Islamic only by virtue of a conscious application of the sociopolitical tenets of Islam to the life of the nation, and by an incorporation of those tenets in the basic constitution of the country.

But, then, one might ask: Does Islam *really* expect the Muslims to strive, at all times and under all circumstances, for the establishment of an Islamic state—or is the desire for it based only on their historical memories? Is Islam *really* so constituted that it demands of its followers a definite course of political, communal action—or does it perhaps leave, as other religions do, all political action to be decided by the people themselves in the light of the exigencies of the times? In short, is the "mixing of religion with politics" a genuine postulate of Islam, or not?

The intimate connection between religion and politics which is so characteristic of Muslim history is, more often than not, somewhat unpalatable to modern, Western-educated Muslims who have grown accustomed to considering questions of belief and of practical life as belonging to entirely separate realms. On the other hand, it is impossible to gain a correct appreciation of Islam without paying full attention to this problem. Anyone who is acquainted, however superficially, with the teachings of Islam knows that they not only circumscribe man's relation to God, but also lay down a definite scheme of social behavior to be adopted in result of that relation. Starting from the fundamental assumption that all aspects of natural life have been God-willed and possess, therefore, a positive value of their own, the Qur'ān makes it abundantly clear that the ultimate purpose of all creation is the compliance of the created with the will of the Creator. In the case of man, this compliance—called *islām*—is postulated as a conscious, active coördination of man's desires and behavior with the rules of life decreed by the Creator. This demand presupposes that—at least with reference to human life—the concepts of "right" and "wrong" have meanings that do not change from case to case or from time to time but retain their validity for all times and all conditions. Obviously, no definitions of "right" and "wrong" arrived at through our speculation can ever possess such eternal validity, for all human thought is essentially subjective and, therefore, strongly influenced by the thinker's time and environment. Hence, if it is really the purpose of religion to guide man toward a coördination of his desires and his behavior with the will of God, he must be taught in unmistakable terms how to differentiate between good and evil and, consequently, what to do and what not to do. A mere general instruction in ethics—such as "love your fellow men," "be truthful," "put your trust in God"—does not suffice, because it is subject to many conflicting interpretations. What is needed is a precise body of laws which would outline, however broadly, the whole sphere of human life in all its aspects—spiritual, physical, individual, social, economic, and political.

Islam fulfills this need by means of a Divine Law—called *sharīʿah*—which has been provided in the ordinances of the Qurʾān and supplemented (or, rather, detailed and exemplified) by the Prophet Muhammad in the body of teachings which we describe as his *sunnah*, or way of life. From the viewpoint of the believer, the Qurʾān and the Sunnah reveal to us a conceptually understandable segment of God's all-embracing plan of creation. With reference to man, they contain the only available positive indication of what God wants us to be and to do.

But He only *indicates* His will to us: He does not *compel* us to behave in the way indicated. He gives us freedom of choice. We may, if we so desire, willingly submit to His revealed Law and thus, as it were, coöperate with Him; and we may, if we choose, go against Him, disregard His Law, and risk the consequences. However we decide, the responsibility is ours. It goes without saying that our ability to lead an Islamic life depends on our making the former choice. Nevertheless, even if we choose to obey God, we may not always be able to do it fully: for although it is obvious that the innermost purpose of Islamic Law is man's righteousness in the individual sense, it is equally obvious that a good deal of that Law can become effective only through a consciously coördinated effort of many individuals—that is, through a communal effort. From this it follows that an individual, however well-intentioned he may be, cannot possibly mold his private existence in accordance with the demands of Islam unless and until the society around him agrees to subject its practical affairs to the pattern visualized by Islam. So conscious a coöperation cannot arise out of a mere *feeling* of brotherhood: the concept of brotherhood must be translated into positive social action—the "enjoining of what is right and forbidding of what is wrong" (*al-amr bi 'l-ma-'rūf wa 'n-nahy 'an al-munkar*)—or, to phrase it differently, the creation and maintenance of such social conditions as would enable the greatest possible number of human beings to live in harmony, freedom, and dignity. Now, it is obvious that anti-social behavior on the part of one person may make it difficult for other persons to realize this ideal; and the larger the number of such "rebels," the greater the difficulty for the rest. In other words, the community's willingness to coöperate in terms of Islam must remain largely theoretical so long as there is no worldly power responsible for enforcing Islamic Law and preventing rebellious behavior—at least in matters of social concern—on the part of any of the community's members. This responsibility can be discharged only by a coördinating agency invested with the powers of command (*amr*) and prohibition (*nahy*): that is, the state. It follows, therefore, that the organization of an Islamic state or states is an indispensable condition of Islamic life in the true sense of the word.

Why Not a "Secular" State?

There is no doubt that countless Muslims passionately desire a sociopolitical development on Islamic lines; but there is also no doubt that in the mental climate of the modern world it has become almost axiomatic among many educated people that religion ought not to interfere with political life. And, while the principle of "secularism" is automatically identified with "progress," every suggestion to consider practical politics and socioeconomic planning under the aspect of religion is dismissed out of hand as reactionary or, at best, as "impractical idealism." Apparently, many educated Muslims share this view today; and in this, as in so many other phases of our contemporary life, the influence of Western thought is unmistakable.

For reasons of their own, the people of the West have become disappointed with religion (their religion), and this disappointment is reflected in the ethical, social, and political chaos now pervading a large part of the world. Instead of submitting their decisions and actions to the criterion of a moral law—which is the ultimate aim of every higher religion—these people have come to regard expediency (in the short-term, practical connotation of the word) as the only obligation to which public affairs should be subjected; and because the ideas as to what is expedient naturally differ in every group, nation, and community, the most bewildering conflicts of interest have come to the fore in the political field, both national and international. For, obviously, what appears to be expedient from a purely practical point of view to one group or nation need not be expedient to another group or nation. Thus, unless men submit their endeavors to the guidance of an objective, moral consideration, their respective interests must clash at some point or other; and the more they struggle against one another, the wider their interests diverge and the more antagonistic become their ideas as to what is right and what is wrong in the dealings of men.

Briefly, in a modern "secular" state there is no stable norm by which to judge between good and evil, and between right and wrong. The only possible criterion is the "nation's interest." But in the absence of an objective scale of moral values, different groups of people—even within one nation—may have, and usually do have, widely divergent views as to what constitutes the nation's best interests. While a capitalist may quite sincerely believe that civilization will perish if economic liberalism is superseded by socialism, a socialist is as sincerely of the opinion that the very maintenance of civilization depends on the abolition of capitalism and its supersession by socialism. Both make their ethical views—that is to say, the views as to what should and what should not be done to and with human beings—dependent solely on their economic views, with the resultant chaos in their mutual relations.

It has become evident that none of the contemporary Western political systems—economic liberalism, communism, national socialism, social democracy, and so forth—is able to transform that chaos into something resembling order: simply because none of them has ever made a serious attempt to consider political and social problems in the light of absolute moral principles. Instead, each of these systems bases its conception of right and wrong on nothing but the supposed interests of this or that class or group or nation—in other words, on people's changeable (and, indeed, continuously changing) material preferences. If we were to admit that this is a natural—and therefore desirable—state of man's affairs, we would admit, by implication, that the terms "right" and "wrong" have no real validity of their own but are merely convenient fictions, fashioned exclusively by time and socioeconomic circumstances. In logical pursuance of this thought, one would have no choice but to deny the existence of any moral obligation in human life: for the very concept of moral obligation becomes meaningless if it is not conceived as something absolute. As soon as we become convinced that our views about right and wrong or good and evil are only man-made, changeable products of social convention and environment, we cannot possibly use them as reliable guides in our affairs; and so, in planning those affairs, we gradually learn to dispense with all moral guidance and to rely on expediency alone—which, in turn, leads to ever-growing dissensions within and between human groups and to a progressive decrease in the amount of happiness vouchsafed to man. This is, perhaps, the ultimate explanation of the deep disquiet which is apparent throughout the modern world.

No nation or community can know happiness unless and until it is truly united from within; and no nation or community can be truly united from within unless it achieves a large degree of unanimity as to what is right and what is wrong in the affairs of men; and no such unanimity is possible unless the nation or community agrees on a moral obligation arising from a permanent, absolute moral law. Obviously, it is *religion* alone that can provide such a law and, with it, the basis for an agreement, within any one group, on a moral obligation binding on all members of that group.

Religion and Morality

Whatever the particular tenets of this or that religion, however sublime or primitive its teachings, whether monotheistic, polytheistic, or pantheistic, the innermost core of every religious experience—at all periods of history and in all civilizations—is, first, man's inner conviction that all being and happening in this world is the outcome of a conscious, creative, all-embracing Power—or, to put it more simply, a Divine Will; and, second, the feeling that one is, or at least ought to be, in spiritual accord with that Will. On this feeling and this conviction alone was and is based man's faculty to judge between good and evil. For, unless we presume that an absolute, planning Will is at the root of all creation, there is no sense in our presuming that any of our aims and actions could be intrinsically right or wrong, moral or immoral. In the absence of a belief in such a planning Will, all our concepts of morality must of necessity become vague and more and more subject to expediency: that is, subject to the question of whether or not an aim or an action is useful (in the practical sense of the word) to the person concerned or to the community to which he belongs. Consequently, "right" and "wrong" become purely relative terms, to be interpreted arbitrarily according to one's personal or communal needs, which, in their turn, are subject to the continuous changes in one's socioeconomic environment.

These reflections on the role of religious thought and feeling in the realm of morality assume a paramount importance if we realize that the trend of our time is definitely antagonistic to religion as such. Everywhere and every day we are being told by a certain class of intellectuals that religion is nothing but a relic of man's barbaric past, which is now allegedly being superseded by the "Age of Science." Science, they say, is about to take the place of the worn-out, outmoded religious systems; science, so gloriously and irresistibly growing, will at last teach man to live in accordance with "pure reason," and will in time enable him to evolve new standards of morality without any metaphysical sanction.

This naïve optimism with regard to science is in reality not at all "modern": it is, on the contrary, extremely old-fashioned — an uncritical copy of the Occident's naïve optimism of the eighteenth and nineteenth centuries. During that period (and particularly in the second half of the nineteenth century), many Western scientists believed that a solution of the mysteries of the universe was "just around the corner," and that henceforward nothing would stop man from arranging his life in God-like independence and reasonableness. The thinkers of our time, however, are much more reserved—not to say skeptical—on this subject. Under the tremendous impact of modern, twentieth-century physics, contemporary thinkers have come to the conclusion that deterministic science is unable to fulfill the spiritual hopes attached to it as recently as a hundred or even fifty years ago: for they have found that the mysteries of the universe become more mysterious and more complicated the more our research advances. Every day it becomes more obvious that it may never be possible to answer by purely scientific means the questions of how the universe came into being, how life originated in it, and what constitutes the phenomenon of life itself: and, therefore, also the question of the true nature and purpose of human existence. But until we are in a position to answer this last-named question, we cannot even *attempt* to define moral values such as "good" and "evil": simply because such terms have no meaning at all unless they are related to a knowledge (real or imaginary) of the nature and the purpose of human existence.

This is what our most advanced scientists are now beginning to realize. Faced with the impossibility of answering metaphysical questions by means of physical research, they have given up the naïve hope of the last two centuries that science could ever provide directives in the field of ethics and morality. Not that these advanced scientists distrust science as such: on the contrary, they do believe that it will lead mankind to ever greater marvels of knowledge and achievement; but at the same time they realize that scientific endeavor has no direct connection with man's moral and spiritual life. No doubt, science can, and does, guide us to a better understanding of the world around and within us; but, being solely concerned with the observation of the facts of nature, and with the analysis of the laws that appear to govern the interrelation of those facts, it cannot be called upon to deliver a verdict as to the purpose of human life and, thus, to provide us with valid directives as to the social behavior we ought to adopt. It is only indirectly, through speculative reasoning on the basis of certain established facts, that science can attempt to advise us in this respect. But because science is always in a state of flux—always subject to the discovery of new facts of nature and, consequently, to an unceasing reinterpretation and revaluation of previously ascertained sets of facts—its advice is hesitant, spasmodic, and, at times, quite contradictory to previously tendered advice: which, in a nutshell, amounts to saying that science is never in a position to lay down with certainty what man should do or leave undone in order to achieve well-being and happiness. And for this reason science cannot (nor does it really attempt to) foster moral consciousness in man. In short, the problems of ethics and morality are not within the scope of science. They are, on the other hand, entirely within the scope of religion.

It is through religious experience alone that we can arrive—rightly or wrongly—at standards of moral valuation independent of the ephemeral changes in our environment. I have said "rightly or wrongly" because, by all objective canons of reasoning, there is always the possibility of a religion (any religion) being mistaken in its metaphysical premises and, consequently, in the moral valuation deduced from those premises: thus, our acceptance or rejection of any religion must, in the last resort, be guided by our reason, which tells us how far that particular religion corresponds to man's ultimate needs, both physical and spiritual. But this necessity of exerting our critical faculties with regard to the teachings of a religion does not detract anything from the fundamental proposition that it is religion alone that can endow our life with meaning and thus promote in us the urge to conform our thinking and our behavior to a pattern of moral values entirely independent of the momentary constellation of our individual existence. To phrase it differently, only religion can provide a broad platform for an agreement among large groups of men as to what is good (and therefore desirable) and what is evil (and therefore to be avoided). And could there be any doubt that such an agreement is an absolute, indispensable requirement for any sort of order in human relations?

Considered from this viewpoint, the religious urge in man is not a mere passing phase in the history of his spiritual development, but the ultimate source of all his ethical thought and all his concepts of morality; not the outcome of primitive credulity which a more "enlightened" age could outgrow, but the only answer to a real, basic need of man at all times and in all environments. In another word, it is an *instinct*.

It is reasonable, therefore, to presume that a state built on the foundations of religion offers an infinitely better prospect of national happiness than a state founded upon the concept of a "secular" political organism; provided, of course, that the religious doctrine on which such a state rests—and from which it derives its authority—makes full allowance, first, for man's biological and social needs, and, second, for the law of historical and intellectual evolution to which human society as a whole is subject. The first of these two conditions can be fulfilled only if the religious doctrine in question attributes positive value not only to man's spiritual nature but also to his biological nature—as Islam undoubtedly does. The second condition can be fulfilled if the political law that is to guide the community's behavior is not only concrete and self-evident but also free from all rigidity—which is, precisely, what we claim for the political law laid down in Qur'ān and Sunnah.

In the following pages I shall try to substantiate this claim. But before proceeding with this task, I find it necessary, in view of the lack of agreement among Muslim scholars as to the extent and the details of *shar*ʿ*ī* legislation, to make a few general observations about the concept of Islamic Law as such.

The Scope of Islamic Law

As is well known, not all the laws which form the subject matter of conventional Muslim jurisprudence (*fiqh*) rest on injunctions expressed in clear-cut terms of command and prohibition in Qur'ān and Sunnah. By far the larger part of *fiqhī* rulings are the outcome of various deductive methods of reasoning, among which *qiyās* (deduction through analogy) figures most prominently. The great *fuqahā'* (jurists) of the past arrived at their legal findings on the basis of their study of Qur'ān and Sunnah, and there is no doubt that in the instance of the foremost exponents of *fiqh* this study was extremely deep and conscientious. Nevertheless, the results of such studies were often highly subjective: that is, they were determined by each scholar's personal approach to, and interpretation of, the legal sources of Islam, as well as by the social and intellectual environment of his age. Because that environment was in many respects vastly different from ours, some of these "deductive" conclusions naturally differ from the conclusions we might reach at the present time: which is one of the reasons why so many modern Muslims are reluctant to apply the rulings devised by conventional *fiqh* to contemporary problems of politics and economics.

Originally, all such rulings were intended by their authors to facilitate the application of *shar'ī* principles to specific questions. In the course of time, however, these rulings acquired in the popular mind a kind of sacrosanct validity of their own and came to be regarded by many Muslims as an integral part of the *sharī'ah*, the Canon Law, itself. In support of this popular view, it is argued that the explicit legal statements, commands, and prohibitions contained in the Qur'ān and the authenticated Traditions (*aḥādīth*) recording the sayings and doings of the Prophet are, by themselves, not sufficient to circumscribe all possible legal situations, and that, therefore, an amplification of the *corpus juris* by means of deductive reasoning is necessary. However, quite apart from the fact that neither Qur'ān nor Sunnah offers the slightest warrant for such an arbitrary enlargement of the *sharīʿah*, one might with justice argue (as a considerable number of Muslim scholars have argued through the centuries) that the limited scope of the explicit ordinances contained in Qur'ān and Sunnah was not due to an oversight on the part of the Law-Giver but, on the contrary, was meant to provide a most essential, deliberate safeguard against legal and social rigidity: in short, it is reasonable to assume that the Law-Giver never intended the *sharīʿah* to cover in detail all conceivable exigencies of life. He intended no more and no less than to stake out, as it were, the legal boundaries within which the community ought to develop, leaving the enormous multitude of "possible" legal situations to be decided from case to case in accordance with the requirements of the time and of changing social conditions.

Thus, the true *sharīʿah* is far more concise and very much smaller in volume than the legal structure evolved through the *fiqh* of various schools of Islamic thought. Being a Divine Law, the *sharīʿah* cannot possibly have been made dependent on scholarly deductions or inferences of a subjective nature, but must be considered to have been laid down in its entirety in the definite ordinances of Qur'ān and Sunnah—ordinances expressed in positive terms of law: "do this," "do not do that," "such-and-such a thing is right, and therefore desirable," "such-and-such a thing is wrong, and therefore to be shunned." These ordinances are described technically as *nuṣūṣ* (singular, *naṣṣ*). By their very nature, they are not subject to conflicting interpretations; in fact, they are in no need of any "interpretation" whatsoever, being absolutely self-contained and unambiguous in their wording. All Arab philologists agree that "the *naṣṣ* of Qur'ān and Sunnah denotes the ordinances [*aḥkām*] forthcoming from the self-evident [*ẓāhir*] wording in which they are expressed."[1] All such *naṣṣ* ordinances are so formulated that they can be applied to every stage of man's social and intellectual development; on the other hand, many of the subjective conclusions of the *fuqahā'* are reflections of a particular time and mentality and cannot, therefore, lay claim to eternal

[1] *Lisān al-ʿArab*, Beirut, 1957 (1375 A.H.), Vol. VII, p. 98.

validity. Thus, it is the *nuṣūṣ* of Qur'ān and Sunnah—and only these—that collectively constitute the real, eternal *sharīʿah* of Islam. This *sharīʿah* concerns itself exclusively with what the Law-Giver has ordained in unmistakable terms as an obligation or put out of bounds as unlawful; whereas the far larger area of things and activities which the Law-Giver has left unspecified—neither enjoining nor forbidding them in *naṣṣ* terms—must be regarded as allowable (*mubāḥ*) from the *sharʿī* point of view.

The reader should not suppose that the views propounded above are an innovation in Islamic thought. In point of fact, they were held by the Companions of the Prophet and, later, by some of the greatest scholars of Islam—and particularly by the man who may rightly be considered one of the most brilliant *fuqahā'* in all our history: Ibn Ḥazm of Cordova (384–456 A.H.) [A.D.994–1064]. Nothing could be more illustrative of the problem under discussion than the following passages from the Introduction to his great work, *Al-Muḥallā*:

> The *sharīʿah* in its entirety refers either to obligatory acts [*farḍ*], the omission of which constitutes a sin; or to forbidden acts [*ḥarām*], the commission of which constitutes a sin; or to allowed acts [*mubāḥ*], the commission or omission of which does not make man a sinner. Now these *mubāḥ* acts are of three kinds: first, acts which have been recommended [*mandūb*] —meaning that there is merit in doing them, but no sin in omitting them; second, acts which are undesirable [*makrūh*]—meaning that there is merit in abstaining from them, but no sin in committing them; and, third, acts which have been left unspecified [*muṭlaq*]—being neither meritorious nor sinful whether committed or omitted...
>
> The Apostle of God said: "Do not ask me about matters which I have left unspoken: for, behold, there were people before you who went to their doom because they had put too many questions to their prophets and thereupon disagreed [about their teachings]. Therefore, if I command you any-

> thing, do of it as much as you are able to do; and if I forbid you anything, abstain from it."[2]
>
> The above Tradition circumscribes all the principles of religious law [*dīn*] from the first to the last. It shows that whatever the Prophet has left unspoken—neither ordering nor forbidding it—is allowed [*mubāḥ*], that is, neither forbidden nor obligatory. Whatever he ordered is obligatory [*farḍ*], and whatever he forbade is unlawful [*ḥarām*]; and whatever he ordered us to do is binding on us to the extent of our ability alone.[3]

Because it is restricted to commands and prohibitions expressed in self-evident terms in Qur'ān and Sunnah, the real *sharī'ah* is extremely concise and, therefore, easily understandable; and because it is so small in volume, it cannot—nor, as I have pointed out, was it ever intended to—provide detailed legislation for every contingency of life. Consequently, the Law-Giver meant us Muslims to provide for the necessary, additional legislation through the exercise of our *ijtihād* (independent reasoning) in consonance with the spirit of Islam. It must, of course, be understood that any *ijtihādī* legislation we may evolve under the inspiration of Qur'ān and Sunnah (occasionally even with the help of the *ijtihād* of past generations) will always be subject to amendment by the *ijtihād* of those who will come after us: that is to say, it can amount to no more than a temporal, changeable law subject to the authority of the irrevocable, unchangeable *sharī'ah*, which is self-evident in the *nuṣūṣ* of Qur'ān and Sunnah.

The *sharī'ah* cannot be changed, because it is a Divine Law; and it need not be changed, because all its ordinances are so formulated that none of them ever conflicts with the real nature of man and the genuine requirements of human society at any time: simply because it legislates only with regard to those aspects

[2] Muslim, on the authority of Abū Hurayrah.

[3] Abū Muḥammad 'Alī ibn Ḥazm, *Al-Muḥallā* (Cairo; 1347 A.H.), Vol. I, pp. 62-64.

of human life which by their very nature are not subject to change. This special characteristic of the Divine Law—its applicability to all stages and conditions of human development—presupposes that its ordinances cover, in the first instance, general principles only (allowing thereby for the necessity of time-conditioned variations in matters of detail), and, in the second instance, provide for detailed legislation in such matters as are not affected by changes due to man's social development. On examining the context of the *nuṣūṣ*, it will be found that this assumption is correct. Whenever detailed *naṣṣ* legislation is forthcoming, it invariably relates to such aspects of our individual and social existence as are independent of all time-conditioned changes (for example, the basic elements of human nature and of human relations). Whenever, on the other hand, changes are indispensable for human progress (for example, in matters of government, technology, economic legislation, and so forth), the *sharīʿah* does not stipulate any detailed laws, but either lays down general principles only or refrains from making any legal enactment. And this is where *ijtihādī* legislation rightfully comes in. To be more precise, the legitimate field of the community's lawmaking activity comprises (*a*) details in cases and situations where the *sharīʿah* provides a general principle but no detailed ruling, and (*b*) principles *and* details with regard to matters which are *mubāḥ*, that is, not covered by *sharʿī* laws at all. It is this method that the Qur'ān has referred to in the words:

لكل جعلنا منكم شرعة ومنهاجاً

"For every one of you We have ordained a Divine Law and an open road."[4] Thus, while the Divine Law (the *sharīʿah*) outlines the area within which Muslim life may develop, the Law-Giver has conceded to us, within this area, an "open road" (*minhāj*) for temporal legislation which would cover the contingencies deliberately left untouched by the *nuṣūṣ* of Qur'ān and Sunnah.

[4] Qur'ān 5:48.

The Need for Free Inquiry

A rediscovery of the "open road" of Islam is urgently required at a time like this, when the Muslim world finds itself in the throes of a cultural crisis which may affirm or deny, for centuries to come, the validity of Islam as a practical proposition. Set as we are in the midst of a rapidly changing world, our society, too, is subject to the same inexorable law of change. Whether we like it or not, a change there will be—it is, indeed, already being enacted before our eyes: a fact as evident as it is pregnant with tremendous possibilities for better of for worse. For better or for worse: this phrase merits emphasis because we must not forget that "change" is but another word for "movement" and, within a social organism, movement can be creative as well as destructive. From the Islamic point of view, an endeavor to return to the realities of Qur'ān and Sunnah, and to find on their basis new channels for our political thought and our social actions, is a movement of the first-named kind. The present drift of Muslim society toward Western concepts and institutions is a movement of the second kind. We can, if it suits us, continue on this drift and thus allow Islam to be gradually obliterated as an independent factor of civilization; and we can, if we so desire, make a new start in terms of the sociopolitical program of Islam and thereby resurrect our culture from the cold ashes of decay.

However, if we decide on the second alternative, it is not enough to say, "We are Muslims, and have therefore an ideology of our own": we must also be in a position to show to ourselves and to the world that this ideology is vital enough to withstand the pressure of the many adverse social and cultural influences converging upon us from all sides, and that even now it can offer us precise directives for the formation of our polity. In order to be able to do this, we must give up our sterile reliance on what to previous generations of Muslim scholars appeared to be "final" verdicts on the sociopolitical laws of Islam, and must begin to think about them anew, in a creative manner, on the basis of our own study of the original sources.

If we approach our task in this spirit of free inquiry, we shall arrive at two important conclusions. First, the concept of Islamic Law—especially with regard to public law—acquires once again that simplicity which had been envisaged for it by the Law-Giver but has subsequently been buried under many layers of conventional and frequently arbitrary interpretation. Second—and this is most pertinent to the problem before us—the outward forms and functions of an Islamic state need not necessarily correspond to any "historical precedent." All that is required of a state in order that it might deservedly be described as "Islamic" is the embodiment in its constitution and practice of those clear-cut, unambiguous ordinances of Islam which have a direct bearing on the community's social, political, and economic life. As it happens, those ordinances are very few and very precisely formulated; and they are invariably of such a nature as to allow the widest possible latitude to the needs of any particular time and social condition.

Chapter II

TERMINOLOGY AND HISTORICAL PRECEDENT

Misapplication of Western Terms

One of the main reasons for the confusion regarding the idea of the Islamic state is the indiscriminate application—both by the upholders and the critics of this idea—of Western political terms and definitions to the entirely different concept of Islamic polity. Not infrequently we find in the writings of modern Muslims the assertion that "Islamic is democratic" or even that it aims at the establishment of a "socialist" society; whereas many Western writers refer to an alleged "totalitarianism" in Islam which must necessarily result in dictatorship. Such superficial attempts at political definition are not only mutually contradictory, and therefore of no practical value for the purposes of a serious discussion, but also carry with them the danger of looking at the problems of Muslim society from the angle of Western historical experiences alone and, thus, of envisaging developments which may be justifiable or objectionable—depending on the viewpoint of the observer—but may be wholly out of place within the world-view of Islam. One should always remember that when the European or American speaks of "democracy," "liberalism," "socialism," "theocracy," "parliamentary government," and so forth, he uses these terms within the context of Western historical experience. Within this context, such terms have not merely their legitimate place but are also easily understandable: they immediately evoke mental pictures of what has actually happened or might conceivably happen in the course of the West's historical development, and can therefore survive the changes to which the passing of time subjects all human concepts. More than that: the very fact of conceptual change—the fact that many of the political terms current today bear a meaning different from that originally given to them—is ever-present in the mind of a Western thinker; and this awareness confers upon him the ability to view his political terminology as something that is in constant need of revision and readjustment. This flexibility of thought disappears, however, as soon as a political concept is taken over ready-made by people who belong to a very different civilization and have, therefore, passed through different historical experiences. To such people, the political term or institution in question appears, as a rule, to be endowed with an absolute, unchanging meaning which does not take into consideration the fact of its historical evolution and, consequently, contributes to the very rigidity of political thought which the new conceptual acquisition had sought to remove.

Take, for instance, the term "democracy." In the West, it is still largely—though by no means wholly—used in the sense given to it by the French Revolution, namely, the principle of socio-economic equality of all citizens, and of government by the entire adult population through its elected representatives, on the basis of "one person, one vote." In its wider connotation, this term implies the people's unrestricted right to legislate by a majority vote on all matters of public concern. Thus, the "will of the people" is set forth, theoretically at least, as something that is free of all external limitations, sovereign unto itself and responsible only to itself. It is obvious that this concept of democracy is vastly different from that held by the originators of the term—the ancient Greeks. To them, the "rule of, or by, the people" (which is what the word "democracy" connotes) implied a strictly oligarchic form of government. In their city-states, the "people" were synonymous with the "citizens"—that is, the free-born inhabitants of the state, who rarely, if ever, exceeded one-tenth of its total population; all the rest were slaves and serfs who were not permitted to perform any but menial labors and—although they were frequently obliged to render military service—possessed no civic rights at all. Only the thin uppermost layer of the population—the "citizens"—had the right of active and passive franchise, and thus all political power was concentrated in their hands. Viewed from this historical perspective, "democracy" as conceived in the modern West is infinitely nearer to the Islamic than to the ancient Greek concept of liberty; for Islam maintains that all human beings are socially equal and must, therefore, be given the same opportunities for development and self-expression. On the other hand, Islam makes it incumbent upon Muslims to subordinate their decisions to the guidance of the Divine Law revealed in the Qur'ān and exemplified by the Prophet: an obligation which imposes definite limits on the community's right to legislate and denies to the "will of the people" that attribute of sovereignty which forms so integral a part of the Western concept of democracy. A tendency superficially similar to that of Islam can be discerned in the concept of "ideological" democracy prevalent in the USSR and other Communist states. There, as in Islam, an ideology is placed over and above the people's freedom to legislate for themselves; only within the framework of that ideology can the majority vote become effective. However, as just mentioned, this similarity is only superficial: first, because Islam bases all its ideological concepts on a Divine Law which, to the believer, is ethically binding in an absolute, immutable sense, whereas the ideology of communism is admittedly the product of a human doctrine and is therefore subject to the most far-reaching amendments; and, second, because Islam makes the comprehension and interpretation of its Law dependent on the individual's knowledge and conscience alone and does not force him to accept interpretations by any other individual or organized body as morally binding. (Notwithstanding the frequent violations of this principle in the course of Muslim history, the teachings of Islam are unequivocal on this subject.)

From the foregoing it is evident that even in the West the terms "democracy" and "democratic liberties" can be and are being used in widely divergent connotations. Their application—either in an affirmative or in a negative sense—to the political ideology of Islam necessarily produces an atmosphere of vagueness and, with it, a tendency to juggle with words.

The same can be said of many other sociopolitical terms which play a genuine—that is, historically warranted—role in Western thought, but are extremely equivocal with reference to Islamic ideology. One could, for example, assert (as some modern Muslim writers do) that Islam is "socialistic" in its tendencies because it aims at a state of affairs which would ensure to all citizens equality of opportunity, economic security, and an equitable distribution of national wealth; however, one could maintain with the same degree of assurance that Islam is opposed to socialism if it is taken to imply (as Marxian socialism undoubtedly does) a rigid regimentation of all social life, the supremacy of economics over ethics, and the reduction of the individual to the status of a mere economic factor. Even the question as to whether Islam aims at "theocracy" cannot be answered with a simple "yes" or "no." We might say "yes" if by theocracy we mean a social system in which all temporal legislation flows, in the last resort, from what the community considers to be a Divine Law. But the answer must be an emphatic "no" if one identifies theocracy with the endeavor—so well known from the history of medieval Europe—to invest a priestly hierarchy with supreme political power: for the simple reason that in Islam there is no priesthood or clergy and, consequently, no institution equivalent to the Christian Church (that is, an organized body of doctrine and sacramental functions). Since every adult Muslim has the right to perform each and every religious function, no person or group can legitimately claim to possess any special sanctity by virtue of the religious functions entrusted to them. Thus, the term "theocracy" as commonly understood in the West is entirely meaningless within the Islamic environment.

In brief, it is extremely misleading to apply non-Islamic terms to Islamic concepts and institutions. The ideology of Islam has a social orientation peculiar to itself, different in many respects from that of the modern West, and can be successfully interpreted only within its own context and in its own terminology. Any departure from this principle invariably tends to obscure the attitude of Islamic Law toward many of the burning issues of our time.

Islamic Political Forms

The application of non-Islamic terminologies to Islamic concepts of state and government is, however, not the only pitfall in the way of a student of Islamic political law. Perhaps an even greater danger is the reliance of so many Muslims on "historical precedents" as possible guides for our future development.

In the preceding chapter I have stressed one of the basic requirements which any state must fulfill if it is to ensure happiness and well-being to the people that comprise it: namely, to make full allowance for man's social and intellectual evolution and thus avoid rigidity in the concept of political law. Looking back at the past history of Muslim states and at some of the popular, present-day notions regarding the forms and functions of an "ideal" Islamic state, we are able to discern just that element of rigidity which one must deem incompatible with the demands of a healthy social development. I am referring in this connection not merely to ancient Muslim works on political theory which, as a rule, reflect the political conditions obtaining during the ʿAbbāsid period and only too often display an eagerness to gratify the interests of the rulers of the time: I am referring, more particularly, to the idea prevailing among many Muslims, both in the past and in the present, that there could be but *one* form of state deserving the adjective "Islamic"—namely, the form manifested under the four Right-Guided Caliphs—and that any deviation from that model must necessarily detract from the "Islamic" character of the state. Nothing could be more erroneous than this idea.

If we examine objectively the political ordinances of Qurʾān and Sunnah, we find that they do not lay down any *specific* form of state: that is to say, the *sharīʿah* does not prescribe any definite pattern to which an Islamic state must conform, nor does it elaborate in detail a constitutional theory. The political law emerging from the context of Qurʾān and Sunnah is, nevertheless, not an illusion. It is very vivid and concrete inasmuch as it gives us the clear outline of a political scheme capable of realization at all times and under all conditions of human life. But precisely because it was meant to be realized at all times and under all conditions, that scheme has been offered in outline only and not in detail. Man's political, social, and economic needs are time-bound and, therefore, extremely variable. Rigidly fixed enactments and institutions could not possibly do justice to this natural trend toward variation; and so the *sharīʿah* does not attempt the impossible. Being a Divine Ordinance, it duly anticipates the fact of historical evolution, and confronts the believer with no more than a very limited number of broad political principles; beyond that, it leaves a vast field of constitution-making activity, of governmental methods, and of day-to-day legislation to the *ijtihād* of the time concerned.

With reference to the problem before us, one may safely say that there is not only one form of the Islamic state, but many; and it is for the Muslims of every period to discover the form most suitable to their needs—on the condition, of course, that the form and the institutions they choose are in full agreement with the explicit, unequivocal *sharʿī* laws relating to communal life.

These political *sharʿī* laws (which will presently be discussed in detail) found their full expression in the administrative institutions and methods that prevailed at the time of the Right-Guided Caliphs—and therefore their state was Islamic in every sense of the word. However, we must not forget that in the unwritten constitution to which the Islamic Commonwealth conformed in those days, there were, side by side with the explicit *sharʿī* laws relating to statecraft, certain other laws enacted by the rulers of the time in accordance with their own interpretation of the spirit of Qurʾān and Sunnah—that is to say, derived through *ijtihād.* Apart from these, we encounter in the period of the Right-Guided Caliphate many other administrative and legislative enactments which were neither directly nor indirectly derived from Qurʾān or Sunnah but from purely commonsense considerations of governmental efficiency and public interest (as, for example, ʿUmar's establishment of the *dīwān*, or treasury office, after a Persian model, or his prohibiting warriors from Arabia to acquire landed property in the newly conquered territories). Inasmuch as such enactments were promulgated by the legitimate government of the day and were, moreover, not contrary to the spirit or the letter of any *sharʿī* law, they had full legal validity for that time. But this does not mean that they must remain valid for all times.

The Example of the Prophet's Companions

An objection to this claim of legal flexibility might thus be made: "Were not those great Companions of the Prophet better acquainted with the innermost aims of Islam than we could ever be? Is it not, therefore, absolutely necessary to follow their example as closely as possible in matters of statecraft as well? Did not the Apostle of God himself urge us to model our behavior on that of his Companions?"

This objection has an emotional background of great force, and so I shall try to answer it at this stage of our discussion.

It is true that the Prophet has impressed on us the necessity of taking his Companions as an example: not only because they had spent many years in the Master's company and were thus fully aware of his ways, but also because the character and behavior of some of them attained to incomparably high levels. However, our moral obligation to try to emulate the great Companions relates precisely to their character and behavior—to their spiritual and social integrity, their selflessness, their idealism, and their unquestioning surrender to the will of God. It cannot and does not relate to an imitation, by people of later times, of the Companions' procedure in matters of state administration—for the simple reason, pointed out above, that this procedure was in many respects an outcome of time-conditioned requirements and individual *ijtihād*, and did not in each and every instance depend on *sharʿī* ordinances alone. The Prophet's sanction of a ruler's right to resort to such free, *ijtihādī* decisions is illustrated in many Traditions, but perhaps nowhere as lucidly as in the classical report of his conversation with his Companion Muʿādh ibn Jabal:

إن رسول الله (صلعم) لما بعثه إلى اليمن قال : ”كيف تقضى إذا عرض لك
قضاء؟“ قال : ”أقضى بكتاب الله.“ قال : ”فإن لم تجد فى كتاب الله؟“ قال :
فبسنة رسول الله.“ قال : ”فإن لم تجد فى سنة رسول الله؟“ قال : ”أجتهد
برأيي ولا آلو.“ قال : فضرب رسول الله (صلعم) على صدره وقال : ”الحمد لله
الذى وفق رسول رسول الله لما يرضى به رسول الله!“

> When he [Muʿādh ibn Jabal] was being sent [as governor] to the Yemen, the Prophet asked him: "How will you decide the cases that will be brought before you?" Muʿādh replied: "I shall decide them according to the Book of God."—"And if you find nothing concerning [a particular matter] in the Book of God?"—"Then I shall decide it according to the Sunnah of God's Apostle."—"And if you find nothing about it in the Sunnah of God's Apostle?"—"Then," replied Muʿādh, "I shall exercise my own judgment [*ajtahidu bi-raʾyī*] without the least hesitation." Thereupon the Prophet slapped him upon the chest and said: "Praised be God, who has caused the messenger of God's Messenger to please the latter!"[1]

By no stretch of imagination could Muʿādh be supposed to have meant that his—as yet nonexistent—legal or administrative decisions would become a permanent addition to the code of laws enunciated in the *nuṣūṣ* of Qurʾān and Sunnah. Nor could the Prophet have intended to sanction the future *ijtihādī* judgments of Muʿādh as binding on anybody outside the latter's temporal or territorial jurisdiction, not to speak of later generations: for it might well have happened (as indeed it frequently did happen) that a Companion's decision on a particular matter was at variance with the opinions of other Companions. The Prophet's saying implied no more and no less than an approval of his Companion's common sense in claiming for himself the right of an independent decision in all matters not formulated in terms of law in the *nuṣūṣ* of Qurʾān and Sunnah. In point of fact, none of the Companions ever regarded his own *ijtihād*—either on questions of belief or of action—as binding, in a religious sense, on any other person.

1 At-Tirmidhī and Abū Dāʾūd, on the authority of Muʿādh ibn Jabal.

Their hearts were blessed with the deepest humility; and none of them ever arrogated to himself the status of a law-giver for all times. Yet precisely such a status has come to be ascribed to them by people of later generations: by people who in their pious—and certainly justifiable—admiration of those splendid Friends of the Prophet have become blind to the element of imperfection inherent in all human nature. In this blindness they commit the mistake of regarding every detail of the Companions' *ijtihād* in political matters as a "legal precedent" binding on the community for ever and ever: a view justified neither by the *sharīʿah* nor by common sense.

Without in the least impairing our reverence for the Companions, we may safely admit that all findings obtained through *ijtihād*, by however great a person, are invariably conditioned by that person's environment and state of knowledge: and knowledge, especially in matters of social concern, depends not so much on the loftiness of a man's character as on the sum total of the historical experience available to him. There can be no doubt that the historical experience available to us is, without any merit on our part, very much wider than that which was available to the Companions thirteen centuries ago. Indeed, we have only to think of the immense development in the intervening centuries of so many scientific concepts in order to realize that in some respects we are even better equipped to grasp the inner purport of this or that socioeconomic proposition of Islam than the Companions could possibly have been: simply because we can draw not only upon their experiences, but also upon the accumulated historical and intellectual experience of those thirteen centuries which, to them, still lay shrouded in the impenetrable mists of the future.

We should never forget that the message of Islam is eternal and must therefore always remain open to the searching intellect of man. The very greatness of the Qur'ān and of the Prophet's life-example lies in the fact that the more our knowledge of the world progresses, the better we can understand the wisdom of the Law of Islam. Thus, our right to independent *ijtihād* on the basis of Qur'ān and Sunnah is not merely permissive, but mandatory; and particularly so in matters on which the *sharīʿah* is either entirely silent or has given us no more than general principles.

It is obvious that our conclusions as to the best means of achieving administrative efficiency and safeguarding social equity are conditioned by the time and the socioeconomic environment in which we live—and so, logically, quite a big proportion of the legislative enactments in an Islamic state must vary from time to time. This cannot, of course, affect those elements of legislation which are clearly ordained in the *nuṣūṣ* of Qurʾān and Sunnah and are therefore unchangeable from the viewpoint of the believer; nor can it affect the essential proviso that all such variable, non-*sharʿī* enactments must not run counter to existing, unequivocal *sharʿī* injunctions. With all this, however, there can be not the least doubt that an Islamic constitution to be evolved thirteen centuries after the Right-Guided Caliphs may legitmately differ from that which was valid in and for their time.

It is, however, not even necessary to visualize an interval of thirteen centuries in order to understand that the political requirements of one time often differ from the requirements in this respect of an earlier period. Even within the short span of a few decades, the Right-Guided Caliphs themselves varied their system of administration—or, as we would say today, the constitution of the state—in many a point. As an illustration, let us take the problem of choosing the head of the state.

There was, naturally, no difference among the Companions concerning the principle of elective government as such, for, as we shall see, the *sharīʿah* is perfectly clear on this subject. However, although it is beyond doubt that the chief executive of an Islamic state must be elected, the Law does not specify any particular *method* of election; and so, rightly, the Companions regarded the method of election as something that lay outside the scope of the *sharīʿah* and could, therefore, legitimately be varied in accordance with the best interests of the community. Thus, the first Caliph, Abū Bakr, was elected by the chiefs of the *muhājirs* and *anṣār*[2] present at

The *muhājirs* were the Meccan Muslims who accompanied the Prophet on

Medina at the time of the Prophet's demise. On his deathbed, Abū Bakr designated ʿUmar as his successor, and this choice was subsequently ratified by the community (ratification being, in this instance, equivalent to election). When ʿUmar, in his turn, was dying, he nominated an electoral body composed of six of the most prominent Companions of the Prophet and entrusted them with choosing his successor from among themselves. Their choice fell on ʿUthmān, who was thereupon recognized by the community as ʿUmar's rightful successor. After ʿUthmān's death, ʿAlī was proclaimed Caliph by a congregation in the Prophet's Mosque, and the majority of the community thereupon pledged their loyalty to him.

Hence, under each of these four reigns which we describe as "right-guided," the constitution of the state differed on a most important point; for it cannot be denied that the method by which the head of the state is elected is a constitutional question of great importance. The different treatment accorded by the Companions to this question—with regard to both the composition of the electorate and the electoral procedure—shows that, in their opinion, the constitution of the state could be altered from time to time without making it any the less "Islamic" on this account.

Apart from this, it is a mistake to believe that the endeavors of the Right-Guided Caliphs represented the *fulfillment* of all Islamic aims, including those relating to statecraft. Had it been so, Islam would be no more than a call to eternal repetition, for nothing would have been left to us but to imitate the doings of our predecessors. In reality, however, Islam is a call to eternal progress, socially as well as spiritually, and, therefore, also politically.

The Right-Guided Caliphate was a most glorious beginning of Islamic statecraft, never excelled, or even continued, in all the centuries that followed it: but it was, for all that, a beginning only. From the moment of Abū Bakr's accession to the moment of ʿAlī's death, the Islamic Commonwealth was, from the structural point

his *hijrah*, or migration, from Mecca to Medina; the *anṣār* (literally "helpers") were those Medinese who rallied to the Prophet on his arrival in their town.

of view, in a permanent state of change, organically growing and developing with each successive conquest and with each new administrative experience. Within a generation it expanded from the confines of Arabia to an enormous dominion stretching from North Africa deep into Central Asia. A state which in the lifetime of the Prophet embraced only agricultural and pastoral communities with simple needs and comparatively static problems suddenly became the heir to the most complicated Byzantine and Sassanian civilizations. At a time when almost all the energies of the government had to be directed toward military consolidation and ensuring the minimum of administrative efficiency, new, staggering problems were arising every day in the sphere of politics and economics. Governmental decisions had often to be made on the spur of the moment and thus, of necessity, many of them were purely experimental. To stop at that first, splendid experiment and to contemplate, thirteen centuries after the Right-Guided Caliphs, the organization of an Islamic state in exactly the same forms, with exactly the same institutions in which *their* state was manifested, would not be an act of true piety: it would be, rather, a betrayal of the Companions' creative endeavor. They were pioneers and pathfinders, and if we truly wish to emulate them, we must take up their unfinished work and continue it in the same creative spirit. For did not the Prophet say,

أصحابي أمانة لأمتي

"My Companions are a trust committed to my community"?[3]

[3] Muslim, on the authority of Abū Burdah.

Chapter III

GOVERNMENT BY CONSENT AND COUNCIL

The Goals of the Islamic State

The innermost purpose of the Islamic state is to provide a political framework for Muslim unity and coöperation:

اعتصموا بحبل الله جميعاً ولا تفرقوا واذكروا نعمت الله عليكم إذ كنتم أعداء فألف بين قلوبكم فأصبحتم بنعمته إخواناً وكنتم على شفا حفرة من النار فأنقذكم منها. كذلك يبين الله لكم آيته لعلكم تهتدون ولتكن منكم أمة يدعون إلى الخير ويأمرون بالمعروف وينهون عن المنكر وأولئك هم المفلحون.

> Hold fast, all together, to the covenant of God, and do not separate. And remember God's favor unto you—how, when you were enemies, He united your hearts, so that by His favor you became brethren; and how, when you were on the brink of an abyss of fire, He drew you back from it. Thus God makes His messages clear to you, so that you may find guidance, and that out of you may grow a community of people who issue a call to equity, enjoin what is right and forbid what is wrong: and it is these alone that shall attain to everlasting happiness.[1]

Thus, an Islamic state is not a goal or an end in itself but only a means: the goal being the growth of a community of people who stand up for equity and justice, for right and against wrong—or, to put it more precisely, a community of people who work for the creation and maintenance of such social conditions as would enable the greatest possible number of human beings to live, morally as well as physically, in accordance with the natural Law of God, Islam. An indispensable prerequisite for such an achievement is the development of a strong sense of brotherhood among the community. The Qur'ānic words,

[1] Qur'ān 3:103-104.

إنما المؤمنون إخوة

"The Faithful are but brethren,"[2] have been enlarged upon by the Prophet on innumerable occasions:

المؤمن للمؤمن كالبنيان يشد بعضه بعضاً. المسلم أخ المسلم لا يظلمه ولا يسلمه، ومن كان في حاجة أخيه كان الله في حاجته ومن فرج عن مسلم كربة فرج الله عنه كربة من كربات يوم القيامة ومن ستر مسلماً ستره الله يوم القيامة.

> The Faithful are to one another like [parts of] a building—each part strengthening the others.[3] Every Muslim is brother to a Muslim, neither wronging him nor allowing him to be wronged. And if anyone helps his brother in need, God will help him in his own need; and if anyone removes a calamity from [another] Muslim, God will remove from him some of the calamities of the Day of Resurrection; and if anyone shields [another] Muslim from disgrace, God will shield him from disgrace on the Day of Resurrection.[4]

Now what should be the emotional basis of this brotherhood? Certainly not the tribal or national loyalty which in non-Islamic communities supplies the sole *raison d'être* of all political groupment, and which the Prophet scornfully condemned as unworthy of a true believer:

لينتهين أقوام يفتخرون بآبائهم الذين ماتوا، إنما هم ليكونن أهون على الله من الجعل الذي يدهده الخرء بأنفه؛ إن الله قد أذهب عنكم عبية الجاهلية وفخرها بالآباء؛ إنما هو مؤمن تقي أو فاجر شقي، الناس كلهم بنو آدم وآدم من تراب.

> There are indeed people who boast of their dead ancestors; but in the sight of God they are more contemptible than the black beetle that rolls a piece of dung with its nose.[5] Behold, God has removed from you the arrogance of the Time of

[2] Qur'ān 49:10.
[3] Al-Bukhārī and Muslim, on the authority of Abū Mūsā.
[4] *Ibid.*, on the authority of ʿAbd Allāh ibn ʿUmar.
[5] This black beetle (*juʿal*), the size of a small hen's egg, is a common sight in the deserts of Arabia. It collects dry dung and rolls it to its dwelling-hole in the ground.

Ignorance [*jāhiliyyah*] with its boast of ancestral glories. Man is but a God-fearing believer or an unfortunate sinner. All people are the children of Adam, and Adam was created out of dust.[6]

Nationalism in all its forms and disguises runs counter to the fundamental Islamic principle of the equality of all men and must, therefore, be emphatically ruled out as a possible basis of Muslim unity. According to Qur'ān and Sunnah, that unity must be of an ideological nature, transcending all considerations of race and origin: a brotherhood of people bound together by nothing but their consciousness of a common faith and a common moral outlook. In the teachings of Islam, it is such a community of ideals alone that can provide a justifiable basis for all human groupment; whereas, on the other hand, the placing of the real or imaginary interests of one's nation or country above moral considerations has been condemned by the Prophet in the sharpest terms:

ليس منا من دعا إلى عصبية ، وليس منا من قاتل على عصبية ، وليس منا من مات على عصبية .

"He is not of us who proclaims the cause of tribal partisanship; and he is not of us who fights in the cause of tribal partisanship; and he is not of us who dies in the cause of tribal partisanship."[7] When he was asked by one of his Companions to explain the meaning of "tribal partisanship" (*'aṣabiyyah*), which so obviously places a person outside the pale of Islam, the Prophet replied,

أن تعين قومك على الظلم

"[It means] your helping your own people in an unjust cause."[8] On another occasion he made it clear that love of one's own people as such cannot be described as "tribal partisanship" unless it leads to doing wrong to other groups.[9] On the other hand,

6 At-Tirmidhī and Abū Dā'ūd, on the authority of Abū Hurayrah.
7 Abū Dā'ūd, on the authority of Jubayr ibn Muṭ'im.
8 *Ibid.*, on the authority of Wāthilah ibn al-Asqa'.
9 Aḥmad ibn Ḥanbal and Ibn Mājah, on the authority of 'Ubādah ibn Kathīr.

قال رسول الله (صلعم) : "أنصر أخاك ظالماً أو مظلوماً." فقال رجل : "يا رسول الله ! أنصره مظلوماً ، فكيف أنصره ظالماً ؟" قال : "تمنعه عن الظلم ، فذلك نصرك إياه."

"The Apostle of God said: 'Help your brother, be he a wrongdoer or wronged.' Thereupon a man exclaimed: 'O Apostle of God! I may help him if he is wronged; but how could I [be expected to] help a wrongdoer?' The Prophet answered: 'You must prevent him from doing wrong: that will be your help to him.'"[10]

Thus, the prevention of injustice and the establishment of justice on earth are the ultimate objectives of the social message of Islam:

كنتم خير أمة أخرجت للناس تأمرون بالمعروف وتنهون عن المنكر وتؤمنون بالله

"You are the best community that has been sent forth to mankind [in that] you enjoin right and forbid wrong and have faith in God."[11]

It is on this "enjoining of right and forbidding of wrong" that the ethical value of the Muslim community and of Muslim brotherhood depends; it is with this ideal of justice—justice toward Muslims and non-Muslims alike—that the concept of an Islamic state (which is but the political instrument of that ideal) stands and falls.

To make the Law of Islam the law of the land in order that equity may prevail; to arrange social and economic relations in such a way that every individual shall live in freedom and dignity, and shall find as few obstacles as possible and as much encouragement as possible in the development of his personality; to enable all Muslim men and women to realize the ethical goals of Islam not only in their beliefs but also in the practical sphere of their lives; to ensure to all non-Muslim citizens complete physical security as well as complete freedom of religion, of culture, and of social development; to defend the country against attack from without and disruption from within; and to propagate the teachings of Islam to the world at large: it is in these principles, and in these alone, that the concept of an Islamic state finds its meaning and justification. If it real-

10 Al-Bukhārī and Muslim, on the authority of Anas.
11 Qur'ān 3:110.

izes them, the state can rightly be described as "God's vice-gerent on earth"—at least in that part of the earth which falls under its factual jurisdiction.

Guiding Principles

From the *shar'ī* point of view, the legitimacy of an Islamic state—that is to say, its religious claim to a Muslim's loyalty and allegiance—rests on the fundamental injunction of the Qur'ān,

يا أيها الذين آمنوا أطيعوا الله وأطيعوا الرسول وأولى الأمر منكم

"O you Faithful! Obey God and obey the Apostle and those in authority from among you."[12] In this concise manner the Qur'ān establishes several important principles relating to the nature of an Islamic state.

First: The foremost duty of such a state consists in enforcing the ordinances of the *sharī'ah* in the territories under its jurisdiction. This obligation has been further stressed in the verse,

ومن لم يحكم بما أنزل الله فأولئك هم الفاسقون

"Those who do not judge by what God has revealed—those indeed are the evildoers."[13] Hence, no state can be deemed genuinely Islamic unless its constitution contains an enactment to the effect that the laws of the *sharī'ah* bearing on matters of public concern shall form the inviolable basis of all state legislation. I should like to point out that this limitation of state jurisdiction to "matters of public concern" does not, of course, imply that the *sharī'ah* itself could ever be similarly restricted in its scope—for it undoubtedly relates to the whole of man's life, both public and private. We should not, however, lose sight of the fact that the state, being a social organization, is concerned exclusively with the social aspect of human life and, consequently, requires of the *sharī'ah* no more than a code of laws bearing on this aspect.[14]

[12] Qur'ān 4:59.
[13] *Ibid.*, 5:47.
[14] For a suggestion regarding the codification of such *shar'ī* laws, see chapter vi.

Second: Although such a code must forever remain basic in the structure and the working of an Islamic state, it cannot, by its very nature, supply *all* the laws that may be needed for the purposes of administration. Thus, as we have seen, we will have to supplement the *sharʿī* stipulations relating to matters of public concern by temporal, amendable laws of our own making—on the understanding, of course, that we may not legislate in a manner that would run counter to the letter or the spirit of any *sharʿī* law: for,

وما كان لمؤمن ولا مؤمنة إذا قضى الله ورسوله أمراً أن يكون لهم الخيرة من أمرهم

"Whenever God and His Apostle have decided a matter, it is not for a faithful man or woman to follow another course of his or her own choice."[15] Consequently, the constitution must explicitly lay down that no temporal legislation or administrative ruling, be it mandatory or permissive, shall be valid if it is found to contravene any stipulation of the *sharīʿah*.

Third: The Qurʾānic command, "Obey God and obey the Apostle," is immediately followed by the words, "and those in authority from among you"—that is, from among the Muslim community: which amounts to a statement that an imposition of power from outside the Muslim community cannot be morally binding on a Muslim while, on the other hand, obedience to a properly constituted Islamic government is a Muslim's religious duty. Obedience to the government is, of course, a principle of citizenship recognized as fundamental in all civilized communities; but it is important to note that within the context of an Islamic polity this duty remains a duty only so long as the government does not legalize actions forbidden by the *sharīʿah*, or forbid actions which are ordained by it. In such a contingency, obedience to the government ceases to be binding on the community, as clearly stated by the Prophet:

السمع والطاعة على المرء المسلم فيما أحب وكره ما لم يؤمر بمعصية ، فإذا أُمر بمعصية فلا سمع ولا طاعة .

[15] Qurʾān 33:36.

"Hearing and obeying is binding on a Muslim, whether he likes or dislikes the order—so long as he is not ordered to commit a sin; but if he is ordered to commit a sin, there is no hearing and no obeying."[16] In other words, the community's allegiance to "those in authority from among you" is conditional upon those in authority acting in obedience to God and His Apostle. From this principle it follows that the community is duty-bound to supervise the activities of the government, to give its consent to right actions, and to withdraw it whenever the government deviates from the path of good conduct. Thus, government subject to the people's consent is a most essential prerequisite of an Islamic state.

Fourth: The principle of "popular consent" presupposes that the government as such comes into existence on the basis of the people's free choice and is fully representative of this choice. This is yet another aspect of the Qur'ānic expression "from among you." It refers to the community as a whole, and not to any particular group or class within it. It follows that, in order to satisfy the requirements of Islamic Law, the leadership of the state must be of an *elective* nature and that, consequently, any assumption of governmental power through nonelective means—for instance, on the basis of the fictitious "birthright" implied in hereditary kingship—becomes automatically, even though the claimant be a Muslim, as illegal as an imposition of power from outside the Muslim community.[17]

[16] Al-Bukhārī and Muslim, on the authority of Ibn 'Umar.

[17] Some of my readers will, perhaps, object to this categorical condemnation of hereditary kingship by pointing to the frequent occurrence of the term *sulṭān*—nowadays popularly equated with "king"—in several authentic Traditions dealing with political problems. As a matter of fact, the use of this very expression by the Prophet has for centuries supplied a convenient excuse for the quite un-Islamic institution of hereditary monarchy. This excuse is, however, entirely invalid. In classical Arabic—the language of the Qur'ān and the Traditions—*sulṭān* denotes primarily "a proof" or "a convincing argument"; in its secondary sense, "authority" or "power" in both its abstract and concrete meanings. Whenever the Prophet spoke of "*sulṭān*" in the context of the community's political life, he invariably applied this term to what we today describe as "government"; and this was the practice of his Companions as well. The application of the term to a *person* entrusted with government—that

The Source of State Sovereignty

This brings us to the question (interesting from the viewpoint of political philosophy) of the sources from which an Islamic state is supposed to derive its sovereignty: a question not nearly as "theoretical" as it might appear at first glance.

To be sure, the individual average citizen does not, as a rule, concern himself unduly with speculation as to the "sources of state sovereignty" so long as the institutions and the administrative procedure of the state have or seem to have a favorable effect on his personal mode of living and on the possibilities of his economic advancement. Nevertheless, no historian can deny that the moral values which the citizens attribute to their state are, in the long run, decisive for the survival of its spiritual authority and thus, ultimately, for the survival of social discipline in the widest sense of the word. No outward political forms, even the best of them, can achieve their objective by themselves. Their usefulness depends, in the last resort, on their spiritual contents; and if those contents are defective, the consequences may well be disastrous for the community. Thus, it is highly probable that the centuries-old lack of social discipline and civic spirit among the Muslim community is largely due to the confusion (in its own turn caused by a series of unfortunate historical developments) regarding the conceptual basis of the authority inherent in the state as such. This confusion might perhaps explain the meekness with which the Muslims have for centuries submitted to every kind of oppression and exploitation at the hands of unscrupulous rulers.

Obviously, the political climate of our time no longer favors such a meek submission to injustice. Under the influence of Western political theories, more and more educated Muslims have begun to assert that ultimate sovereignty belongs to "the people," whose will alone must be decisive in the formation of all state

is, a ruler or a king—is definitely a post-classical corruption of the original meaning. (See, for instance, Lane's *Arabic-English Lexicon*, Part 4, pp. 1405-1406).

institutions as well as in the scope of current legislation. Even among those modern Muslims who accept in principle the idea of an Islamic state, there are an appreciable number who claim absolute sovereignty for the "united will of the people" (*ijmāʿ*) on the basis of the Prophet's saying,

إن الله لا يجمع أمتي على ضلالة

"Never will God make my community agree on a wrong course."[18]

Many Muslims conclude from this Tradition that whatever the community—or at least the majority within it—agrees upon must, under all circumstances, be the right course.[19] But this conclusion is entirely unjustified. The above saying of the Prophet is negative, not positive. He meant exactly what he said: namely, that never would all Muslims pursue a wrong course, and that always there would be persons or groups among them who would disagree with the erring ones and would insist on taking the right course.

Therefore, whenever we speak of the "will of the people" in the context of Islamic political thought, we should be careful to avoid what a popular saying describes as "emptying the child with the bath"—in other words, we should not substitute for the un-Islamic autocracy of our past centuries the equally un-Islamic concept of unrestricted sovereignty on the part of the community as a whole.

Inasmuch as the legitimacy of an Islamic state arises from the people's voluntary agreement on a particular ideology and is, moreover, conditional upon their consent to the manner in which the state is administered, one might be tempted to say that "sovereignty rests with the people"; but inasmuch as in a consciously Islamic society the people's consent to a particular method of government and a particular scheme of sociopolitical coöperation is but a result of their having accepted Islam as a Divine Ordinance, there can be

[18] At-Tirmidhī, on the authority of ʿAbd Allāh ibn ʿUmar.

[19] This conclusion is analogous to the ancient Roman saying, *vox populi, vox Dei* ("the voice of the people is the voice of God"), which finds an echo in all Western concepts of democracy.

no question of their being endowed with sovereignty *in their own right*. The Qur'ān says:

قل : اللهم مـٰلك الملك تؤتى الملك من تشآء وتنزع الملك ممن تشآء وتعز من تشآء
وتذل من تشآء ، بيدك الخير ، إنك على كل شىء قدير .

> Say: O God, Lord of Sovereignty! Thou givest sovereignty to whom Thou pleasest, and takest away sovereignty from whom Thou pleasest. Thou exaltest whom Thou pleasest, and abasest whom Thou pleasest. In Thy hand is all good: for Thou hast power over all things.[20]

Thus, the real source of all sovereignty is the will of God as manifested in the ordinances of the *sharīʿah*. The power of the Muslim community is of a vicarious kind, being held, as it were, in trust from God; and so the Islamic state—which, as we have seen, owes its existence to the will of the people and is subject to control by them—derives its sovereignty, ultimately, from God. If it conforms to the *sharʿī* conditions on which I have dwelt in the preceding pages, it has a claim to the allegiance of its citizens in consonance with the words of the Prophet:

من أطاعنى فقـد أطاع الله ومن عصانى فقـد عصى الله ، ومن يطع الأمير فقد
أطاعنى ومن يعصى الأمير فقد عصانى .

"He who obeys me, obeys God; and he who disobeys me, disobeys God. And he who obeys the *amīr* [i.e., the head of the state], obeys me; and he who disobeys the *amīr*, disobeys me."[21] Thus, when the majority of the community have decided to entrust the government to a particular leader, every Muslim citizen must consider himself morally bound by that decision even if it goes against his personal preferences.

The Head of the State

Since the purpose of an Islamic state is not "self-determination" for a racial or cultural entity but the establishment of Islamic Law as a

[20] Qur'ān 3:26.
[21] Al-Bukhārī and Muslim, on the authority of Abū Hurayrah.

practical proposition in man's affairs, it is obvious that only a person who believes in the Divine origin of that Law—in a word, a Muslim—may be entrusted with the office of head of the state. Just as there can be no fully Islamic life without an Islamic state, no state can be termed truly Islamic unless it is administered by people who can be supposed to submit willingly to the Divine Law of Islam.

This principle would naturally cause no difficulty in countries populated entirely or almost entirely by Muslims (as, for instance, Saudi Arabia and Afghanistan). But in those Muslim countries which contain appreciable non-Muslim minorities—and the majority of Muslim countries fall within this category—the above demand may cause some apprehension inasmuch as it would seem to imply a discrimination between Muslim and non-Muslim citizens. To be sure, this fear of discrimination relates only to the theory and not to the practice of government: for in countries where Muslims form an overwhelming majority (and only these can justifiably be termed "Muslim countries"), the leadership of the state automatically accrues to them. Nevertheless, in the context of modern political thought, which is so strongly influenced by Western concepts and prejudices, even a theoretical discrimination on the ground of religion might be unpalatable to many Muslims, not to mention the non-Muslim minorities living in their midst. One must, therefore, frankly admit from the outset that without a certain amount of differentiation between Muslim and non-Muslim there can be no question of our ever having an Islamic state or states in the sense envisaged in Qur'ān and Sunnah. Consequently, any prevarication on this subject is utterly dishonest with regard to both the non-Muslim world around us and the Muslim community itself.

This does not and cannot mean that we should discriminate against non-Muslim citizens in the ordinary spheres of life. On the contrary, they must be accorded all the freedom and protection which a Muslim citizen can legitimately claim: only they may not be entrusted with the key position of leadership. One cannot escape the fact that no non-Muslim citizen—however great his personal integrity and his loyalty to the state—could, on psychological grounds, ever be supposed to work wholeheartedly for the ideological objectives of Islam; nor, in fairness, could such a demand be made of him. On the other hand, no ideological organization (whether based on religious or other doctrines) can afford to entrust the direction of its affairs to persons not professing its ideology. Is it, for instance, conceivable that a non-Communist could be given a political key position—not to speak of supreme leadership of the state—in Soviet Russia? Obviously not, and logically so: for as long as communism supplies the ideological basis of the state, only persons who identify themselves unreservedly with its aims can be relied upon to translate those aims into terms of administrative policy.

The above finding, taken in conjunction with the *naṣṣ* ordinance,

أطيعوا الله وأطيعوا الرسول وأولى الأمر منكم

"Obey God and obey the Apostle and those in authority from among you," leads us inescapably to the conclusion that those who are to wield supreme authority in the Islamic state and are to be responsible for the shaping of its policies should always be Muslims: and this not merely *de facto*, by virtue of their majority in the country, but also *de jure*, by virtue of a constitutional enactment. If we are resolved to make Islam the dominant factor in our lives, we must have the moral courage to declare openly that we are not prepared to endanger our future by falling into line with the demands of that spurious "liberalism" which refuses to attribute any importance to men's religious convictions; and that, on the contrary, the beliefs a man holds are far more important to us than the mere accident of his having been born or naturalized in our country.

It is obvious, then, that the head of an Islamic state must be a Muslim. In consonance with the principle enunciated in the Qur'ān,

إن أكرمكم عند الله أتقاكم

"Behold, the noblest of you before God is the most righteous of you,"[22] he must be chosen on merit alone; and this precludes any considerations of race, family origin, or previous social status. The Prophet said:

أسمعوا وأطيعوا وإن أمر عليكم عبد حبشى كأن رأسه زبيبة

"Hear and obey, even though your *amīr* be an Abyssinian slave with crinkly hair."[23]

Apart from the stipulation that the prospective *amīr*[24] be a Muslim and the "most righteous of you"—which obviously implies that he must be mature, wise, and superior in character—the *sharīʿah* does not specify any further conditions for eligibility to this office, nor does it lay down any particular mode of election, or circumscribe the extent of the electorate. Consequently, these details are to be devised by the community in accordance with its best interests and the exigencies of the time. The same applies to the question of the period during which the *amīr* shall hold office. It is conceivable that a definite number of years may be fixed for this purpose (possibly with the right to reëlection); alternatively, the *amīr*'s tenure of office may be subject to termination when the incumbent reaches a certain age limit, provided he discharges his duties loyally and efficiently; or, as a third alternative, the tenure of office may be for life, with the same proviso as above—that is to say, the *amīr* would have to relinquish his office only if and when it becomes evident that he does not loyally perform his duties or that he is no longer able to maintain efficiency owing to bodily ill-health or mental debility. In this wide latitude regarding the tenure of the *amīr*'s office we see another illustration of the great flexibility inherent in the political law of Qurʾān and Sunnah.

[22] Qur'ān 49:13.

[23] Al-Bukhārī, on the authority of Anas.

[24] I am using here the designation *amīr* (which may be translated as "commander," "leader," or "holder of authority") for the sake of convenience alone. Although it is one of the two designations used most frequently by the Prophet when referring to the head of the community (the other being *imām*), the Muslims are under no *sharʿī* obligation to adopt this title in preference to any other.

The Principle of Consultation

As we have seen, the *sharīʿah* refrains deliberately from providing detailed regulations for all the manifold, changing requirements of our social existence. The need for continuous, temporal legislation is, therefore, self-evident. In an Islamic state, this legislation would relate to the many problems of administration not touched upon by the *sharīʿah* at all, as well as the problems with regard to which the *sharīʿah* has provided general principles but no detailed laws. In either instance it is up to the community to evolve the relevant, detailed legislation through an exercise of independent reasoning (*ijtihād*) in consonance with the spirit of Islamic Law and the best interests of the nation. It goes without saying that in matters affecting the communal side of our life no legislative *ijtihādī* decisions can possibly be left to the discretion of individuals: they must be based on a definite consensus (*ijmāʿ*) of the whole community (which, of course, does not preclude the community's agreement, in any matter under consideration, on an *ijtihādī* finding arrived at previously by an individual scholar or a group of scholars).

Who is to enact this temporal, communal legislation? Obviously, the community as a whole cannot be expected to sit together and to legislate; and so there must be a person or a limited number of persons to whom the community could delegate its legislative powers and whose decisions would be binding on all. The question is, thus, to what person or persons should this task be entrusted?

Many Muslims are of the opinion—seemingly justified by the example of the Right-Guided Caliphate—that all powers pertaining to temporal, non-*sharʿī* legislation should be vested in one person, namely, the *amīr*: for, having been freely elected by the community, he may be deemed to represent the community not only in executive but also in legislative concerns. However, many other Muslims hold the view—also supported by historical evidence—that so great an accumulation of power in one man's hands is always fraught with the gravest of risks. For one thing, an individual, however brilliant, righteous and well-intentioned, may easily commit mistakes of judgment owing to personal bias in this or that matter; whereas, on the other hand, in an assembly composed of many persons, the very existence of contrasting opinions—and the ensuing debate on these opinions—tends to illuminate every problem from various angles: thus, the danger of individual bias obtruding itself on legislation is, if not eliminated, at least greatly reduced. Nor is this all. Possession of absolute power often corrupts its possessor and tempts him to abuse it, consciously or unconsciously, in his own interest or in that of his partisans. In accordance with this view, the legislative powers of the state should be vested in a body of legislators whom the community would elect for this specific purpose.

It would thus appear that the Muslims are free to make their choice between an autocratic rule exercised by the *amīr* on the one hand, and a rule by council (or assembly, or parliament, or whatever name we may give to it), on the other. But when we examine this question more closely, we find that in reality the apparent freedom of choice between these two alternatives is nonexistent, the issue having been decided most categorically by the Qur'ānic ordinance,

أمرهم شورى بينهم

"Their [the Believers'] communal business [*amr*] is to be [transacted in] consultation among themselves."[25]

This *naṣṣ* injunction must be regarded as the fundamental, operative clause of all Islamic thought relating to statecraft. It is so comprehensive that it reaches out into almost every department of political life, and it is so self-expressive and unequivocal that no attempt at arbitrary interpretation can change its purport. The word *amr* in this injunction refers to all affairs of a communal nature and therefore also to the manner in which the government of an Islamic state is to be established: that is, to the elective principle underlying all governmental authority. Beyond that, the phrase *amruhum shūrā baynahum*—literally, "their communal

[25] Qur'ān 42:38.

business *is* consultation among themselves"—makes the transaction of all political business not only consequent upon, but synonymous with, consultation: which means that the legislative powers of the state must be vested in an assembly chosen by the community specifically for this purpose.

Elective Assembly

It is evident from the context that the expression "among themselves" in the Qur'ānic ordinance under consideration refers to the whole community: hence, the legislative assembly—or, to use a term well known throughout Muslim history, the *majlis ash-shūrā*—must be truly representative of the entire community, both men and women. Such a representative character can be achieved only through free and general elections: therefore, the members of the *majlis* must be elected by means of the widest possible suffrage, including both men and women. The extent of that suffrage and the qualifications to be demanded of the voters—like those of the candidates—are details regarding which neither Qur'ān nor Sunnah provides any clear-cut legislation, and which, consequently, are left to the discretion of the community in the light of the requirements of the time.

One could, of course, argue that, instead of being elected—directly or indirectly—by the whole community, the *majlis* might be sufficiently representative if its members were simply nominated by the *amīr*—because, owing as he does his position and authority to a popular mandate, he might be deemed to be an embodiment of the community's will. But whatever support may be invoked for this view from Muslim history, its weakness at once becomes apparent if we bear in mind that the *manner* in which a legislative body comes into being must be counted among the most important affairs of state; and if we accept the Divine dictum that all our communal affairs are to be transacted on the basis of popular consultation, we cannot escape the conclusion that the process of constituting the *majlis* must be, in itself, an outcome of "consultation" in the widest and most direct sense of the word. In complex societies like ours, such a consultation can take no form other than that of elections during which the merits of the respective candidates are publicly discussed and the votes cast accordingly. The method of elections—direct or indirect, transferable or non-transferable vote, regional or proportional representation, and so forth—has not been laid down in the *sharīʿah* and is, therefore, a matter for communal decision.

One important point, however, has been clearly stipulated by the Prophet with regard to all public appointments and, thus, with regard to elective appointments as well: the prohibition of self-canvassing. The Prophet said:

لا تسأل الإمارة ، فإنك إن أعطيتها عن مسئلة وُكّلت إليها ، وإن أعطيتها عن غير مسئلة أعنت عليها .

"Do not solicit an office of authority [*imārah*], for if it is given to you for the asking, you will be left therein to your own resources, while, if it is given to you without asking, you will be aided [by God] therein."[26] In the light of the teachings of Islam, the Prophet obviously implied that in order to be adequate to one's responsibilities, one must be aided therein by God; on the other hand, lack of Divine aid must necessarily result in failure, however great one's personal resources. To make his point clear, the Prophet consistently refused to make any administrative appointment whenever the person concerned asked for it. For instance, when he was approached by one of his Companions with the request for a government post, he answered emphatically:

إنّا والله لا نولى على هذا العمل أحداً سأله ولا أحداً حرص عليه

"By God, we do not appoint to such work anyone who asks for it, nor anyone who covets it."[27]

Thus, it would be in full keeping with the spirit of the *sharīʿah* if the constitution of an Islamic state would explicitly declare that self-canvassing by any person desirous of being appointed to an

[26] Al-Bukhārī and Muslim, on the authority of ʿAbd ar-Raḥmān ibn Samurah.
[27] *Ibid.*, on the authority of Abū Mūsā.

administrative post (including that of head of the state) or of being elected to a representative assembly shall automatically disqualify that person from being elected or appointed. Such an enactment would immediately remove a weighty objection on the part of many contemporary Muslims to a "government by council." At present anyone possessing local influence or wealth may—regardless of his real worth—secure his election to a legislative assembly by exercising a certain amount of "persuasion" on his electors; but under the above-mentioned enactment, all such attempts at direct persuasion would lead to immediate disqualification. It would, of course, still be possible for an influential but otherwise worthless candidate to avoid the outward appearance of self-canvassing by making use of a party organization or of individual middlemen who would make propaganda for him among the public. However, the fact that the candidate himself would be debarred from delivering electioneering speeches or from otherwise addressing the electorate in his own behalf would make the task extremely difficult: with the result that, as a rule, only a person enjoying well-deserved and unsolicited esteem among the electorate would have a genuine chance of success.

Differences of Opinion

It has already been mentioned that the legislative work of the *majlis ash-shūrā* will relate only to matters of public concern, and more particularly to matters which have not been regulated in terms of law by the *nuṣūṣ* of Qur'ān and Sunnah. Whenever the interests of the community call for a legislative enactment, the *majlis* must first look into the context of the *sharī'ah* for a guiding general principle of law bearing on the problem under consideration. If such a general principle is forthcoming, it falls within the scope of the legislature to draw up an enactment in consonance with the established *shar'ī* principle. But very often the *majlis* will be confronted with problems on which the *sharī'ah* is entirely silent: problems, that is, for which neither detailed rulings nor even a general principle have been formulated in the *nuṣūṣ*. In such instances it is for the *majlis* to devise the requisite legislation, taking only the spirit of Islam and the community's welfare into consideration.

All this presupposes, of course, that the members of the *majlis* are not only possessed of a good working knowledge of the *nuṣūṣ* of Qur'ān and Sunnah, but are also people of understanding and insight (*ūlu 'l-albāb*), alive to the sociological requirements of the community and worldly affairs in general: in other words, education and maturity are indispensable qualifications for election to the *majlis ash-shūrā*.

But even if the members of the *majlis* possess these qualifications, it is highly improbable that they will always view a given social situation in exactly the same light and, consequently, reach full unanimity as to the legislative measures required to meet that situation. This diversity of views is only natural, for all human reasoning is a highly subjective process and can never be fully dissociated from the thinker's temperamental leanings, habits, social background, and past experiences: in brief, from all the manifold influences which act together in the shaping of what we describe as a "human personality." However, true progress is not possible without such a variety of opinions, for it is only through the friction of variously constituted intellects and through the stimulating effect they have on one another that social problems are gradually clarified and thus brought within the range of solution.

It is this that the Prophet had in mind when he said:

إختلاف علماء أمتى رحمة

"The differences of opinion among the learned within my community are [a sign of] God's grace."[28] We should not, therefore, be perturbed by the certain expectation that the decisions of the *majlis ash-shūrā* in an Islamic state—like those of other legislative assemblies the world over—will hardly ever be established through a unanimous vote. The only thing we may legitimately

[28] As-Suyūṭī, *Al-Jāmiʿ aṣ-ṣaghīr*.

expect will be decisions obtained on the majority principle—preferably a simple majority in respect of ordinary legislation, and perhaps a two-thirds majority in questions of exceptional importance, such as a demand for deposition of the government (to be discussed later), amendment of the constitution, declaration of war, and so forth.

In view of the obvious shortcomings of most of the so-called "democratic" systems prevailing in the modern West, some contemporary Muslims dislike the idea of making the legislative activities in an Islamic state dependent on a mere counting of votes. The bare fact, so they argue, that a legislative measure has been supported by a majority does not necessarily imply that it is a "right" measure: for it is always possible that the majority, however large and even well-intentioned, is on occasion mistaken, while the minority—in spite of its being a minority—is right.

The objective truth of this view cannot be disputed. The human mind is extremely fallible; moreover, men do not always follow the promptings of right and equity; and the history of the world is full of instances of wrong decisions made by a foolish or selfish majority in spite of the warnings of a wiser minority. Nevertheless, it is difficult to see what alternative there could be, within a legislative body, to the principle of majority decisions. Who is to establish, from case to case, whether the majority or the minority is right? Whose opinion shall prevail? One might, of course, suggest that the final verdict should rest with the *amīr*; but—quite apart from the fact that the granting of such absolute power to any one person militates against the principle of *amruhum shūrā baynahum* so strongly insisted upon by the Law of Islam—is it not equally possible that the *amīr* is mistaken, while the view of the majority is right? Is there any Divine guarantee attached to his views? To this, the critics of the majority principle usually give the answer: "When we are about to elect the *amīr*, we must see to it that the wisest and most righteous person is chosen; and the very fact of his having been chosen on the grounds of his superior wisdom and righteousness should be guarantee enough that his decisions will be right." Quite true: but is it not equally true that the Muslims are supposed to elect the *majlis ash-shūrā* on the basis of the wisdom and the righteousness attributable to each candidate? Is this not "guarantee enough" that the decisions arrived at by the majority of these legislators will always be correct? Of course not. In either instance—whether in that of the *amīr* or of the *majlis*—"guarantee enough" can never be a substitute for perfect guarantee; and this is, unfortunately, beyond human reach. The best we can hope for is that when an assembly composed of reasonable persons discusses a problem, the majority of them will finally agree upon a decision which in all probability will be right. It is for this reason that the Prophet strongly, and on many occasions, admonished the Muslims:

اتبعوا السواد الأعظم

"Follow the largest group,"[29] and,

عليكم بالجماعة والعامة

"It is your duty to stand by the united community and the majority [*al-ʿāmmah*]."[30]

In fact, human ingenuity has not evolved a better method for corporate decisions than the majority principle. No doubt, a majority can err; but so can a minority. From whatever angle we view the matter, the fallibility of the human mind makes the committing of errors an inescapable factor of human life; and so we have no choice but to learn through trial and error and subsequent correction.

[29] Ibn Mājah, on the authority of ʿAbd Allāh ibn ʿUmar.
[30] Aḥmad ibn Ḥanbal, on the authority of Muʿādh ibn Jabal.

Chapter IV

RELATIONSHIP BETWEEN EXECUTIVE AND LEGISLATURE

Interdependence of Functions

The principle of "consultation among themselves" underlying the creation of the *majlis ash-shūrā* naturally includes the *amīr* among the legislators; for, having been elected by the community as head of the state, he must be regarded as its foremost representative in all matters pertaining to communal business. More than that: by virtue of his being the focal point of all *amr* in an Islamic polity, the *amīr* cannot be merely an ordinary member of the *majlis*, but must be its leader, duty-bound to guide its activities and to preside—either personally or through a delegate—over its deliberations. This stipulation, implying as it does the idea that in a state subject to the authority of a Divine Law there can be no radical separation of the legislative and the executive phases of government, constitutes a most important, specifically Islamic contribution to political theory.

In the democratic states of the West, a sharply drawn division between legislature and executive is considered to be the only effective safeguard against a possible abuse of power by the executive. This Western principle of government has certain merits: for by according to the legislature the attribute of "sovereignty" and thus placing it in a position of control over the day-to-day working of the executive, the latter is undoubtedly held in check and prevented from exercising its power in an irresponsible manner. However, equally undoubtedly, the government as a whole—in both its executive and legislative aspects—is more often than not (and especially in times of national emergency, when executive decisions have to be rapid) greatly hampered by this radical separation of functions, and is thus obviously at a disadvantage vis-à-vis states governed autocratically. Islam, as we know, is as uncompromisingly opposed to autocracy as any of the Western democratic polities could conceivably be: but in this, as in so many other matters, Islam follows a "middle way," avoiding the disadvantages of either of these systems and securing to the Muslim community the advantages of both. By integrating the executive and the legislative phases of government through the instrumentality of the *amīr* (whose function as president of the legislative assembly has been made a necessary corollary of his executive function as head of state), we can fruitfully overcome that duality of power which in Europe and America so often places the executive and the legislature in opposition to one another, and at times makes parliamentary government unwieldy or even ineffectual. But this gain in efficiency (normally so characteristic of "totalitarian," autocratic governments) is, in an Islamic state, not achieved at the cost of relinquishing the principle of popular control over the activities of the government. Indeed, any possible tendency toward autocracy on the part of the executive is checked at the outset by the stipulation, *amruhum shūrā baynahum*, which means that the transaction of *all* governmental activities, executive as well as legislative, must be an outcome of consultation among the accredited representatives of the community.

In logical pursuance of this principle of interdependence, we must conclude that the decisions arrived at by the *majlis ash-shūrā* through a majority vote are not of a merely advisory character—to be accepted or rejected by the holders of executive power at their discretion—but are *legally binding* on them.

A Historical Analysis

We know that at the time of the four Right-Guided Caliphs there was no legislative assembly in the modern sense of this term. To be sure, those great Caliphs did consult the leaders of the community on all outstanding problems of policy; but neither were the persons thus consulted properly "elected" by the community for this purpose, nor did the Caliph feel himself bound in every instance to follow the advice tendered. He asked for advice, considered it on its merits, and thereupon made his decision in accordance with what *he* thought right—sometimes accepting the opinion of the majority, sometimes that of the minority, and sometimes overruling both. One might, therefore, be tempted to ask: If the Right-Guided Caliphs, who had been among the most intimate Companions of the Prophet, did not consider it necessary to have a properly elected council or to follow implicitly the advice of whatever council there was, how can anyone claim today (*a*) that the *majlis ash-shūrā* of an Islamic state must be constituted on the basis of popular elections, and (*b*) that the legislation obtained in such a *majlis* is under all circumstances binding on the executive?

It is comparatively easy to answer the first part of the above question. When the first Caliph, Abū Bakr, was confronted with the necessity—dictated by the Qur'ānic principle, *amruhum shūrā baynahum*—of having a council which would assist him in governing the state, he instinctively turned to an institution that was sanctioned by immemorial custom and had not been repudiated by the *sharī'ah*, namely, an assembly of tribal chiefs and leaders of clans. In the circumstances, the Caliph's choice was undoubtedly correct, for in spite of the considerable loosening of tribal ties brought about by Islam, those ties had not yet been discarded. The Arabian society of that time had preserved its tribal structure to a very large extent, and so the leaders of tribes and clans did in fact, if not in law, possess the authority to speak and act in the name of the groups they represented. The views on communal matters expressed by, say, the leader of the Banū Zuhrah clan of Quraysh or of the *anṣārī* tribe of Aws were almost always identical with the views held by all other members of those clans or tribes. Had the Caliph insisted on elections, it would invariably have been those very chieftains (most of whom had been Companions of the Prophet) whom the community would have designated as its representatives: hence, there was no need to call for elections. All that the Caliph had to do was to summon the outstanding Companions and tribal chiefs—and there was his *majlis ash-shūrā*, as representative of the community as it ever could have been under the conditions then prevailing. This structural peculiarity of Muslim society remained practically unchanged throughout the reign of the four Right-Guided Caliphs, with the result that none of them saw any reason for changing the method by which the council came into being.

However, modern Muslim society (like most other civilized societies) has long since outgrown the tribal mode of life, with the result that clan leadership has lost its erstwhile importance. Consequently, we have no longer any way of ascertaining the opinions of the community except by means of a popular vote. In matters of outstanding importance, this vote may take the shape of a referendum; in matters of day-to-day legislation, nobody has as yet devised a better method than elections: that is, the free appointment by the community of a number of persons who would act as its representatives. This is so obvious that I would not have dwelt on it were it not for the fact that so many Muslims have not yet grasped the structural difference (a most far-reaching difference) between our present society and that which existed in the early days of Islam. Faced with conditions similar to ours, the Right-Guided Caliphs would certainly have reached political conclusions vastly different from those they reached thirteen centuries ago; in other words, they would have had their *majlis* elected through popular vote.

This finding applies not only to the method by which the *majlis* should come into being, but also to the terms of reference under which it would work and the position which it should occupy within the framework of a modern Islamic state—more specifically, to the question of whether or not the legislative decisions of the *majlis* should be binding on the executive.

It is historically established that the Prophet himself frequently called for and followed the advice of his Companions in matters of state, and this in obedience to the words of the Qur'ān,

وشاورهم فى الأمر فإذا عزمت فتوكل على الله

"Take counsel with them in all communal business [*amr*]; and when you have decided on a course of action, place your trust in God."[1] Some Muslim scholars conclude from the wording of this verse that the leader of the community, although obliged to take counsel, is nevertheless free to act thereupon in whatever way he deems fit; but the arbitrariness of this conclusion becomes obvious as soon as we recall that this Qur'ān verse was revealed just before the Battle of Uḥud—that is, on an occasion when the Prophet felt constrained, against his own better judgment, to defer to the advice of the majority of his Companions. He was definitely of the opinion—subsequently justified by events—that the Muslims should not meet the numerically superior army of the Meccan Quraysh in the open field, but should fall back behind the fortifications of Medina instead. In this view he was supported by several of his Companions; but as most of the others insisted on going forth and offering battle, he sorrowfully gave way to the will of the majority.

The *shar'ī* obligation on the part of the leader to follow the decisions of the majority of his council is further elucidated in a Tradition on the authority of the fourth Caliph, 'Alī, relating to the Qur'ān verse we are now considering. When the Prophet was asked about the implications of the word *'azm* (deciding upon a course of action) which occurs in this verse, he answered:

مشاورة أهل الرأى ثم اتباعهم

"[It means] taking counsel with knowledgeable people [*ahl ar-ra'y*] and following them therein."[2] To Abū Bakr and 'Umar, who often constituted what we would describe today as his "inner council," the Prophet once said:

لو اجتمعتما فى مشورة ما خالفتكما

"If you two agree on a counsel, I shall not dissent from you."[3]

[1] Qur'ān 3:159.
[2] Ibn Kathīr, *Tafsīr* (Cairo; 1343 A.H.), Vol. II, p. 277.
[3] Imām Aḥmad ibn Ḥanbal, *Musnad*, on the authority of 'Abd ar-Raḥmān ibn Ghanam.

Nevertheless, it is not difficult to guess why the Right-Guided Caliphs occasionally deviated from this strict observance of the principle, *amruhum shūrā baynahum.* For one thing, the rapidly changing aspect of the Islamic Commonwealth (to which reference has been made in chapter ii) made it sometimes impossible to leave the final decision in matters of state to people who, however well-meaning and wise, could not be supposed to be currently informed about everything that was going on in the wide and continuously expanding realm. Furthermore, the Right-Guided Caliphs were fully aware that political consciousness among the general run of Muslims was still in its infancy and that, consequently, there was always a danger that political views might be colored by considerations of tribal interest; and so, although they established councils and called for advice whenever the need arose, they held themselves free to accept or to reject the advice of their consultants. Most probably this was the only course open to them at the time. Still, it is just possible that so unfettered a freedom of decision on the part of the head of the state was one of the factors contributing to the rapid decay of the Caliphate; for although it led to admirable results in the case of an exceedingly strong and farsighted personality like ʿUmar, it brought the institution of the Caliphate itself into discredit whenever a weaker ruler committed a serious error of judgment. Might not, perhaps, the entire Muslim history have taken a different course if, for instance, ʿUthmān had held himself bound (in the legal sense of the word) always to follow the decisions of a properly constituted *majlis ash-shūrā*?

Whatever answer may be given to this hypothetical question, we are certainly not justified to expect that every *amīr* would possess the genius and the strength of purpose of an ʿUmar. On the contrary, all history shows that such personalities are extremely rare exceptions, and that the vast majority of administrators, at all times and in all societies, are prone to commit grievous errors if left entirely to their own devices. Hence, they should not be left to their own devices, and should be allowed to govern only in consultation with the accredited representatives of the whole community: which is one of the classical lessons of history that no nation may neglect except at its own peril.

Executive Powers

Thus, we have come to the conclusion that an Islamic state must be governed by means of consultation: that is to say, by means of an intimate collaboration between the legislature and the executive (the leadership of both being vested in one and the same person, namely, the *amīr*). But what is to be the technical relationship between these two branches of government? Does the principle according to which all government business must be an outcome of consultation (*amruhum shūrā baynahum*) place on the executive an obligation to submit every detail of day-to-day administration to the prior consent of the legislature? If this were so, no governmental machinery could ever work efficiently: a state of affairs that could not possibly have been countenanced by the *sharī'ah*. It is, therefore, to the *sharī'ah* that we must turn for an answer to this dilemma. And an answer is, indeed, forthcoming from the Qur'ān itself.

We have already had occasion to consider the Qur'ān verse that says,

وشاورهم فى الأمر فإذا عزمت فتوكل على الله

"Take counsel with them in all communal business; and when you have decided upon a course of action, place your trust in God."[4] From this verse we have concluded that the *amīr* is under an obligation to accept the decisions of the *majlis ash-shūrā* as binding on him; but the phrase, "and when you have decided upon a course of action, place your trust in God," leads us to a further conclusion. Whenever the Qur'ān or the Prophet speak of the necessity of *tawakkul* (placing one's trust in God), they invariably refer to actions that are not strictly circumscribed by the available *nuṣūṣ* and call, therefore, for individual judgment as to the manner in which they are to be performed—in other words, they refer to

[4] Qur'ān 3:159.

actions that allow the person concerned a certain latitude of choice subject to the dictates of his conscience. With reference to the problem we are discussing here, this finding could be summed up thus: Although the *amīr* is bound by the temporal legislation enacted by the *majlis ash-shūrā* and by its decisions on major questions of policy, the manner in which he translates those decisions and directives into terms of day-to-day administration is left to the discretion of the executive over which he presides; and although the *majlis*, on the other hand, is empowered to frame the temporal laws on the basis of which the country is to be governed, to decide the major policies which are to be pursued, and in a general way to supervise the activities of the government, it is not entitled to interfere with the day-to-day working of the executive. From this it follows that the *amīr* must possess executive powers within the fullest meaning of these words. An office of head of state shorn of all real power and reduced to a mere figurehead—as, for example, that of the president of pre-Gaullist France or the queen of England—is obviously redundant from the viewpoint of the Qur'ānic injunction which makes the Muslims' obedience to "those who hold authority" (*ūlu 'l-amr*) a corollary of their obedience to God and His Apostle.[5]

Structure of Government

However, even if full executive powers are conceded to the *amīr*, the question remains as to whether those powers—and the functions resulting from them—are to be vested in him alone (as is, for instance, the case with the president of the United States), or whether he should exercise them in partnership, as it were, with a cabinet of ministers representing the major parties in the *majlis ash-shūrā* and depending for their tenure of office on this body's vote of confidence. There exists no explicit *shar'ī* enactment in either of these two directions. Nevertheless, from the wording of many authentic Traditions it appears that the Prophet envisaged the concentration of all executive responsibilities in the hands of

[5] See Qur'ān 4:59.

one person (whom he described variously as *amīr* or *imām*) as being the most suitable for the purposes of an Islamic polity. Here are some of these Traditions:

من أطاعنى فقد أطاع الله ومن عصانى فقد عصى الله ، ومن يطع الأمير فقد أطاعنى ومن يعص الأمير فقد عصانى ؛ وإنما الإمام جُنّة يقاتل من ورائه ويتقى به .

> He who obeys me, obeys God; and he who disobeys me, disobeys God. And he who obeys the *amīr*, obeys me; and he who disobeys the *amīr*, disobeys me. Behold, the leader [*al-imām*] is but a shield from behind which the people fight and by which they protect themselves.[6]

ألا كلكم راع وكلكم مسئول عن رعيته ، فالإمام الذى على الناس راع وهو مسئول عن رعيته . . .

> Verily, each of you is a shepherd, and each of you is responsible for his flock. [Thus,] the leader [*imām*] who is placed over the people is a shepherd responsible for his flock...[7]

من بايع إماماً فأعطاه صفقة يده وثمرة قلبه فليطعه إن استطاع ، فإن جاء آخر ينازعه فاضربوا عنق الآخر.

> He who has pledged allegiance to an *imām*, giving him his hand and the fruit of his heart, shall obey him if he can [i.e., as long as he is not ordered to commit a sin]; and if another person tries to usurp the *imām*'s rights, smite that other person's neck.[8]

These and similar sayings of the Prophet are entirely in keeping with his more general command that whenever a group of Muslims are engaged on any work of common importance, one man should be chosen from among them to lead the others.[9] Nevertheless,

[6] Al-Bukhārī and Muslim, on the authority of Abū Hurayrah.

[7] *Ibid.*, on the authority of ʻAbd Allāh ibn ʻUmar.

[8] Muslim, on the authority of ʻAbd Allāh ibn ʻAmr.

[9] Most of the authentic Traditions to this effect have been quoted and analyzed by Muḥammad ibn ʻAlī ash-Shawkānī (died 1255 A.H.) in his classical work *Nayl al-Awṭār* (Cairo; 1344 A.H.), Vol. IX, pp. 157-158.

one might perhaps argue that even a government on the European parliamentary pattern—that is, a cabinet of ministers deriving their mandates from and directly responsible to the legislature—would not necessarily offend against the principle of one-man leadership inasmuch as in an Islamic state the cabinet would be headed by the *amīr* who, as we know, combines in his person the twin functions of head of the state and of prime minister. Common sense, however, tells us that such an arrangement would render the position of the *amīr* highly anomalous. On the one hand, he is supposed to be the executive *dhu 'l-amr* (holder of authority) in his own right, by virtue of a popular election, while, on the other hand, he would have to share his executive responsibilities with a group of ministers individually responsible to the legislature: thus, it would be the parties represented in the *majlis*, and not the *amīr*, who would be the ultimate fount of all executive power in the state. Apart from the fact that such an arrangement would militate against the Islamic concept of leadership, it would result unavoidably in the government's policy being always dependent on a compromise—or, rather, on an unending series of compromises—between various, sometimes conflicting, party programs, and never being able to attain that single-mindedness and inner continuity so essential for an Islamic state.

This principle of compromise between opposing party programs may be necessary—and sometimes even morally justifiable—in communities which are not animated by any definite ideology and are, therefore, bound to subordinate all political decisions to the people's changing views as to what may be the right course of action under given circumstances; but it is certainly out of place in an ideological Islamic state in which the concepts of "right" and "wrong" have a definite connotation and cannot possibly be made dependent on mere expediency. In such a state, not only legislation but also administrative policy must at all times be expressive of the ideology on which the community has agreed beforehand; and this can never come about if the government is obliged to subordinate its day-to-day activity to a consideration of fluctuating party politics. This, of course, does not preclude the existence of "parties" in an Islamic legislature. If freedom of opinion and of criticism is recognized as the citizen's inherent right (as it undoubtedly is in the political concept of Islam), the people must be accorded the freedom to group together, if they so desire, for the purpose of propagating certain sets of views as to what should be the policy of the state on this or that question; and provided those views do not run counter to the ideology on which the state is based—that is, the *sharīʿah*—the parties thus constituted must have the right to argue them in and outside the *majlis ash-shūrā*. However, this freedom to form parties and to advocate their programs should not be allowed to influence the administrative practice of the government—as it necessarily would if the latter were composed of ministers who receive their mandate from, and remain responsible to, the party organizations represented in the *majlis*.

In view of all this, it would seem that a "presidential" system of government, somewhat akin to that practiced in the United States, would correspond more closely to the requirements of an Islamic polity than a "parliamentary" government in which the executive powers are shared by a cabinet jointly and severally responsible to the legislature. In other words, it is the *amīr* alone to whom all administrative powers and functions should be entrusted, and it is he alone who should be responsible to the *majlis*—and through it, to the people—for the policies of the government. The ministers ought to be no more than his administrative assistants or "secretaries," appointed by him at his own discretion and responsible only to him. As a matter of fact, the very term *wazīr* (popularly translated as "minister") which the Prophet used in connection with problems of government denotes a person who helps the head of the state to bear his burdens: in short, an administrative assistant. Thus, for example, the Prophet said:

إذا أراد الله بالأمير خيراً جعل له وزير صدق إن نسى ذكره وإن ذكر أعانه ،
وإذا أراد به غير ذلك جعل له وزير سوء إن نسى لم يذكره وإن ذكر لم يعنه .

If God means well with the *amīr*, He provides for him a

trustworthy assistant [*wazīr*] to remind him whenever he forgets, and to help him whenever he remembers. And if [God] does not mean it well with him, He provides for him an evil assistant, who does not remind him whenever he forgets and does not help him whenever he remembers.[10]

If, therefore, the Muslims adopt for their state or states the one-man method of government—popularly known today as the "American system"—they will but realize a principle indirectly recommended by the Prophet thirteen centuries ago. This alone should weigh heavily with them when they make their final decision; there is, however, yet another argument in favor of the one-man system.

We know that the *ūlu 'l-amr* (holders of authority) in an Islamic state must be Muslims. If the executive powers of government were to be vested in a cabinet of ministers chosen from the legislature on the basis of party representation—as is customary in the Western European parliamentary democracies—it is these ministers who, together with the *amīr*, would constitute the executive *ūlu 'l-amr* by virtue of the mandate they have received from the *majlis*: in which instance the holding of ministerial power by a non-Muslim would contravene the clear-cut *shar'ī* stipulation which reserves the executive leadership of the state to Muslims. Hence, the community would be faced with the alternative of either statutorily debarring non-Muslim citizens from all ministerial posts (which might make it difficult for the non-Muslim minorities to coöperate loyally with the state), or of blandly disregarding a fundamental injunction of the *sharī'ah* (which would strike at the root of the Islamic concept of the state). However, if all executive powers and prerogatives are vested in the *amīr* alone, he would obviously be the sole *dhu 'l-amr* responsible for the activities of his government, whereas the ministers would be no more than his secretaries or administrative assistants whom he would appoint at his will and to whom he would delegate certain tasks inherent in his office. Because they would not be responsible for policy-making, these

[10] Abū Dā'ūd and An-Nasā'ī, on the authority of 'Ā'ishah.

secretaries could not be regarded as *ūlu 'l-amr* in their own right—and so there could be no *shar'ī* objection whatever to appointing a non-Muslim to a cabinet post. This would not only prevent an unfair discrimination against non-Muslim citizens, but, in addition, would make it possible for the government to utilize, on merit alone, all the best talent available in the country.

The mere fact that there are considerable non-Muslim minorities in most of the Muslim countries should, therefore, tip the balance in favor of the so-called presidential system of government.

Integration of Legislature and Executive

With all this, we must never lose sight of the Qur'ānic injunction, *amruhum shūrā baynahum*, which, as we have seen, makes the transaction of all major governmental business directly dependent on consultation. In theory, this requirement may be fully satisfied by the institution of a *majlis ash-shūrā* which would have to give its verdict on all important policy issues as well as evolve the temporal laws under which the country is to be governed. In practice, however, the matter is not as simple as that.

Every student of politics is aware of the fact that, strange as it may sound, it is not the legislative assembly but the executive branches of government that "make" most laws in a modern state. As a rule, any major item of legislation nowadays entails a great deal of expert preparation and research, a thorough knowledge of the social and economic issues involved, and, finally, considerable legal acumen in the formulation of the law or laws to be enacted. It is obvious that such an accumulation of expert knowledge and technical ability cannot be expected of an assembly of persons elected on the basis of a wide suffrage: for the electorate is, naturally, concerned only with the individual merits of the candidates—their social integrity and their reputation for intelligence—and is not in a position to assess each candidate's technical qualifications for law-making. Quite apart from this, the comparatively large number of people of whom a modern parliament is necessarily composed would, by itself, make it exceedingly difficult to study, prepare, and draft any elaborate legal enactment. Consequently, the relevant work of research, preparation, and drafting—and often also of initiating—new legislation becomes, in modern states, the responsibility of the executive. It is in the executive departments of government that most of the major legislative bills are expertly prepared by civil servants trained specially for this purpose, and are thereupon placed before the legislative assembly for discussion, possible amendment, and final decision.

Such a procedure might be entirely satisfactory from the Islamic point of view so far as popular *consent* is concerned—for, obviously, no legislative measure could become law unless and until it has been thoroughly discussed in the *majlis ash-shūrā* and finally approved by it with or without amendments. However, popular consent alone does not constitute the beginning and the end of all Islamic requirements with regard to legislation: the principle of *amruhum shūrā baynahum* categorically demands that all governmental activity (on the legislative as well as on the executive side) should be a direct outcome of consultation. How can this be achieved without hampering the executive branch of the government at every step and thus destroying its freedom of action? To my mind, there is but one solution to this problem.

We know that in all modern parliaments special committees are instituted to deal with particular problems of government: a foreign affairs committee, a national defense committee, a judiciary committee, and so forth. It is before these bodies, selected by the members of the assembly from among themselves, that the executive has from time to time to justify its policies; and it is from them that it has to obtain the initial approval for the manner in which administrative business is conducted: a procedure which naturally simplifies the subsequent debate in the plenary session of the parliament. However, the approval or disapproval of a parliamentary committee—and subsequently of the entire assembly—is usually only a *post factum* verdict on the executive policies of the government: that is to say, the assembly as such (or any of its parliamentary committees) is only in exceptional instances, and almost never from the outset, associated with the current activities of the executive in a way that would fully correspond to the injunction, *amruhum shūrā baynahum.* In logical compliance with this injunction, the parliamentary committees in an Islamic assembly must be fully integrated with the executive and law-drafting activities of the government. This could be achieved by (*a*) restricting the membership of each committee to a very small number, and (*b*) according to each of the committees the function of an advisory council of the minister (or secretary of state) concerned. In this way, all administrative policies and legislative enactments could be elaborated in consultation with the chosen representatives of the people from beginning to end while, at the same time, the government's ability to act would remain unimpaired.

Arbitration between Legislature and Executive

There remains the important question of what to do when there is disagreement between the *majlis ash-shūrā* and the executive. It might sometimes happen that even in spite of an intimate association of its parliamentary committees with the work of the executive, the *majlis* deems it proper to object to a policy or an administrative measure sponsored by the government because, in the opinion of the majority of the assembly, that policy or administrative measure contravenes some of the existing laws, or otherwise infringes upon what the legislators regard as the best interests of the state; just as it is conceivable that on occasion the *amīr* may, for similar reasons, feel conscience-bound to object to a decision reached by the majority in the *majlis.* The resulting conflict of opinions might lead to deadlocks which could not easily be resolved by the means usually employed in such contingencies by European parliamentary democracies: namely, the resignation of the government or dissolution of the parliament, followed by new elections. On the one hand, the executive of an Islamic state—that is, the *amīr*—has been elected by the entire community, which (by the very act of electing him) has pledged itself to "hear and obey" so long as the *amīr* does not govern in deliberate contravention of the

Law of Islam; on the other hand, the *amīr* is not entitled to override or simply to ignore the majority decisions of the *majlis ash-shūrā*. Nor can the latter body claim for itself, as may the "sovereign" assemblies of most Western democracies, the right of withdrawing its confidence from a government that cannot agree with the assembly's decision on a specific issue, but is nevertheless determined to uphold the ethical values and incontrovertible *naṣṣ* ordinances of Islam: for, individually, the members of the *majlis* are bound by the same pledge of allegiance to the *amīr* by which the whole community is bound. Thus, the deadlock becomes seemingly insoluble. But only seemingly—for here, again, the Qur'ān indicates a way out of a dilemma. In chapter iii we considered the Qur'ānic injunction,

أطيعوا الله وأطيعوا الرسول وأولى الأمر منكم

"Obey God and obey the Apostle and those in authority from among you." But this quotation gave us only the first part of the verse. Its second part runs thus:

فإن تنازعتم فى شىء فردوه إلى الله والرسول

"Then, if you disagree in anything, refer it to God and the Apostle."[11] Evidently, therefore, when there is a fundamental difference between the *majlis ash-shūrā* and "those in authority from among you" (i.e., the *amīr*), the point in dispute should be referred by either of the two sides to the arbitration of Qur'ān and Sunnah—or, to be more explicit, to a body of arbitrators who, after an impartial study of the problem, would decide which of the two conflicting views is closer to the spirit of Qur'ān and Sunnah. Hence, the necessity of having an impartial machinery for arbitration—a kind of supreme tribunal concerned with constitutional issues—becomes obvious. This tribunal should have the right and the duty (*a*) to arbitrate in all instances of disagreement between the *amīr* and the *majlis ash-shūrā* referred to the tribunal by either of the two sides, and (*b*) to veto, on its own accord, any legislative

[11] Qur'ān 4:59.

act passed by the *majlis* or any administrative act on the part of the *amīr* which, in the tribunal's considered opinion, offends against a *naṣṣ* ordinance of Qur'ān or Sunnah. In effect, this tribunal should be the guardian of the constitution.

Needless to say, such a tribunal must be composed of the best jurists that can be found in the community—men who have not only mastered the Qur'ān and the science of *ḥadīth* but who are also fully informed on the affairs of the world: for it is only such men that could decide, with as great a degree of certainty as is granted to the human intellect, whether or not a doubtful legislative act of the *majlis* or an administrative act of the *amīr* is in accord with the spirit of Islam.

In order that the composition of this supreme tribunal should be the result of consultation in the *sharʿī* sense, its members might be selected by the *majlis* from a panel of names submitted by the *amīr*, or vice versa. The appointments, it seems to me, should be for lifetime: even if a member's active tenure of office is made subject to an age limit, he should retain his status and be entitled to full pay until the end of his life, and should not be prematurely removable from active service unless he is unable to discharge his duties on account of physical or mental debility, or has become guilty of misconduct (in which case, he would, of course, forfeit his status and emoluments). And, finally, I would suggest that a member, after having once been appointed to a seat on the tribunal, should be statutorily debarred from holding after retirement or resignation any other post in the state, whether elective or appointive, paid or honorary. In this way, the tribunal members would remain free from all further ambition as well as from all temptation to collaborate with any political party or group interest, and would thus be able to achieve the highest possible degree of impartiality in the performance of their duties.

There can, of course, be no assurance that all the members of the tribunal will always agree in their conclusions; and so, again, we are faced with the necessity of resorting to majority decisions whenever unanimity is not obtainable. But whether unanimous or not, a verdict of the tribunal must be regarded as final and binding on all agencies of the state and on the community as a whole, so long as it is not superseded by a later, similarly obtained verdict. This last reservation is important, for it is quite conceivable that another time and even another composition of the tribunal may give rise to a different decision on the same problem: which means no more and no less than that here, too, the doors of *ijtihād* may never be closed.

Chapter V

THE CITIZENS AND THE GOVERNMENT

The Duty of Allegiance

When the *amīr* has been duly elected, he may be considered to have received a pledge of allegiance (*bay'ah*) from the whole community—that is, not only from the majority that had voted for him but also from the minority whose votes had been cast against him: for, in all communal decisions not involving a breach of any *shar'ī* law, the will of the majority is binding on every member of the community. Thus, the Prophet said:

يد الله على الجماعة ، ومن شَذَّ شُذَّ فى النار .   من فارق الجماعة شبراً فقد خلع الإسلام من عنقه .

> The hand of God is upon the community [*al-jamā'ah*]; and he who sets himself apart from it will be set apart in Hellfire.[1] He who departs from the community [*fāraqa 'l-jamā'ah*] by [even] a handspan ceases to be a Muslim [literally, "throws off Islam from his neck"].[2]

Consequently, if the government fulfills the requirements imposed by the *sharī'ah*, its claim to the allegiance of the citizens is absolute. They are bound

على السمع والطاعة فى العسر واليسر والمنشط والمكره

"to hear and to obey, in hardship and in ease, in circumstances pleasant and unpleasant"[3]: in short, they must stand united behind the government and must be prepared to sacrifice for this unity all their private comforts, interests, possessions, and even their lives—for

[1] At-Tirmidhī, on the authority of 'Abd Allāh ibn 'Umar.
[2] Abū Dā'ūd and Aḥmad ibn Ḥanbal, on the authority of Abū Dharr.
[3] Al-Bukhārī and Muslim, on the authority of 'Ubādah ibn aṣ-Ṣāmit.

إن الله اشترى من المؤمنين أنفسهم وأموالهم بأن لهم الجنة

"Behold, God has bought of the Faithful their persons and their possessions, offering them Paradise in return..."[4]

It follows, therefore, that a government ruling in the name of God and His Prophet and in obedience to the Law of Islam has the right to call upon all the resources of the citizens—including their personal possessions and even their lives—whenever the interests of the community and the security of the state demand such an effort. In other words, the government is entitled (*a*) to impose, over and above the *zakāt*-tax immutably laid down in Qur'ān and Sunnah, any additional taxes and levies that may be deemed necessary for the welfare of the community, (*b*) to impose, whenever necessary, restrictions on private ownership of certain kinds of properties, means of production, or natural resources with a view to their being administered by the state as public utilities, and (*c*) to subject all able-bodied citizens to compulsory military service in defense of the state.

The Question of Jihād

Since this book is limited to a consideration of the constitutional principles underlying the concept of the Islamic state, we need not concern ourselves here with the legislative details which would enable the state to impose on its citizens taxes and other economic obligations in accordance with administrative needs. A few words, however, must be said about the citizens' obligation to render military service—an obligation obviously connected with the concept of *jihād*, which, as we know, has been atrociously misinterpreted by almost all non-Muslim critics of Islam and by not a few among the Muslim *fuqahā'* themselves.

The word *jihād* is derived from *jahada*, which means "he strove or exerted himself," namely, against anything that implies evil; thus, for instance, the Prophet described man's struggle against his own passions and weaknesses (*jihād an-nafs*) as the "greatest

[4] Qur'ān 9:111.

jihād."[5] Applied to actual warfare, the term *jihād* has been used in the Qur'ān exclusively to denote a war of defense—defense of man's freedom of religion, of his country, and of the liberty of his community:

أُذن للذين يقاتلون بأنّهم ظلموا – وإن الله على نصرهم لقدير – الذين أخرجوا من ديارهم بغير حق إلا أن يقولوا ربنا الله. ولو لا دفع الله الناس بعضهم ببعض لهدمت صوامع وبيع وصلوات ومساجد يذكر فيها اسم الله كثيرا.

> Permission to fight is given to those against whom war is being wrongfully waged—and God is indeed able to help them—: those who have been unjustly driven from their homes only because they said, "Our Lord is God." And had not God enabled some people to repel others, it is certain that cloisters and churches and synagogues and mosques, in which the name of God is so often extolled, would have been destroyed.[6]

It is to be borne in mind that this is the earliest reference in the Qur'ān to the problem of *jihād*: on this point there is complete agreement in all available Traditions.[7] In the above two verses the Qur'ān lays down the fundamental principle of self-defense against aggression which alone can make a war morally justifiable; and the reference to "cloisters and churches and synagogues and mosques" makes it amply clear that this defense of political and spiritual freedom must be accorded by the Muslims not only to their own community but also to all the non-Muslims living in their midst.

On no account does Islam permit its followers to wage a war of aggression:

وقاتلوا فى سبيل الله الذين يقاتلونكم ولا تعتدوا إن الله لا يحب المعتدين.
وقاتلوهم حتى لا تكون فتنة ويكون الدين لله ، فإن انتهوا فلا عدوان الا على الظالمين.
لا ينهاكم الله عن الذين لم يقاتلوكم فى الدين ولم يخرجوكم من دياركم أن تبروهم وتقسطوا اليهم ، إن الله يحب المقسطين.

[5] See Al-Bayhaqī, *As-Sunan al-kubrā*, on the authority of Jābir ibn 'Abd Allāh.
[6] Qur'ān 22:39-40.
[7] See Ibn Kathīr, *Tafsīr* (Cairo; 1343 A.H.), Vol. V, pp. 592ff.

> Fight in the way of God against those who fight against you, but do not yourselves commit aggression: for, behold, God does not love aggressors.[8] And fight against them until there is no more persecution and men are free to worship God [literally, "and all religion belongs to God"]. But if they desist, then all hostility shall cease, except against the oppressors.[9] With regard to those [of the unbelievers] who have not made war against you on account of [your] religion and have not driven you out of your homes, God does not forbid you to show kindness to them and to deal with them justly: behold, God loves the doers of justice.[10]

It is in the light of these decisive, self-explanatory ordinances of the Qur'ān that all Traditions enjoining *jihād* upon the Muslims must be read. Whenever the Prophet extolled the merits of *jihād*, he referred either to wars that were taking place at the time or to future wars that might fulfill, as his did, the conditions of war laid down in the Qur'ān. Only such wars can be regarded as waged "in the way of God" (a term that is almost invariably found in all Traditions relating to *jihād*), and therefore as justifiable and meritorious from the viewpoint of the *sharī'ah*.

The concept of an Islamic state, based as it is on the teachings of Qur'ān and Sunnah, would automatically preclude the government of such a state from contemplating wars of aggression. Indeed, the government could not legally count on the obedience of its citizens in such instances: for, acting on the principle that if a Muslim "is ordered to commit a sin, there is no hearing and no obeying",[11] the citizens would be perfectly justified in resorting to what is now termed "conscientious objection"—that is, a refusal to bear arms in a morally reprehensible cause. On the other hand, no such objection can ever be valid for a Muslim if he is called upon to defend his country against attack from without or rebellion

[8] Qur'ān 2:190.
[9] *Ibid.*, 2:193.
[10] *Ibid.*, 60:8.
[11] Al-Bukhārī and Muslim, on the authority of 'Abd Allāh ibn 'Umar.

from within: for this is truly a fight "in the way of God," and to die in such a fight means to achieve supreme martyrdom.

In accordance with the teachings of Islam, every able-bodied Muslim is bound to take up arms in *jihād* whenever the freedom of his faith or the political safety of his community is at stake. Those of the Muslims who are physically unable to serve as soldiers must play their part by means of civic efforts and, so far as they are in a position to do so, through financial contributions. In the words of the Prophet,

من جهز غازياً فى سبيل الله فقد غزا ، ومن خلف غازياً فى أهله فقد غزا .

"He who equips a fighter in the way of God with arms is indeed taking part in the fight; and he who takes care of the family which a fighter has left behind is indeed taking part in the fight."[12] On the other hand,

من لم يغز ولم يجهز غازياً أو يخلف فى أهله بخير أصابه الله بقارعة قبل يوم القيامة

"He who does not fight [himself], nor equips a fighter with arms, nor takes care of the family a fighter has left behind, will be afflicted by God with distress even before the Day of Resurrection [i.e., during his lifetime]."[13] Thus, all adult members of the community are expected to participate in the effort of repelling the enemy; and it is for the agencies of the state to coördinate all the individual endeavors and to weld them into a general system of defense in accordance with the needs of the time.

But what about the non-Muslim citizens?—for, obviously, in the light of the Qur'anic principle,

لا إكراه فى الدين

"There shall be no compulsion in religion,"[14] the religious commandments of Islam cannot be binding upon non-Muslims.

The answer is self-evident. If the authorities in an Islamic state

[12] Al-Bukhārī and Muslim, on the authority of Zayd ibn Khālid.
[13] Abū Dā'ūd, on the authority of Abū Umāmah.
[14] Qur'ān 2:256.

keep strictly to the Qur'ānic concept of *jihād*, which makes war permissible only in self-defense, the duty of defending the state which affords them protection is obviously a duty for the non-Muslim citizens as well; and the more so in view of the fact that Islam extends this protection not merely to their material concerns but also to their spiritual freedom.[15] It is true that the Prophet never insisted that the non-Muslims living under Muslim protection (*ahl adh-dhimmah*) should actively participate in the campaigns which he waged in the defense of Islam; but neither did he forbid non-Muslims to take part in war side by side with the Muslims, if they so desired. The difference between Muslim and non-Muslim in this respect is that the former is bound by the commandments of his *religion* to sacrifice his life, if necessary, in a just war (and only a just war can be called *jihād*), whereas the non-Muslim citizen cannot under all circumstances be called upon to do the same. It may be presumed that the great majority of non-Muslim citizens would be willing, and even eager, to play their part in the defense of a state that offers them full protection and guarantees all their civic rights: still, it is conceivable that some of these non-Muslims —especially Christians—might regard the bearing of arms as incompatible with their religious beliefs and, consequently, object to being drafted for military service; and to such "conscientious objectors" would naturally apply the ordinance, "There shall be no compulsion in religion." They are entitled to exemption from military service on the payment of a special tax, called *jizyah* (which, as its very name denotes, is a "compensation tax," namely, in lieu of military service). No fixed rate has been set by the Prophet for this tax, but from all available Traditions it is evident that it is to be lower than the *zakāt*-tax to which the Muslims are liable and which—because it is a specifically Islamic religious duty —is naturally not levied on non-Muslims. Only those of the non-Muslims who, if they were Muslims, would be expected to serve in the armed forces of the state (and from among them only those who are financially capable) are liable to the payment of *jizyah*.

[15] See the Qur'ānic verse 22:40, quoted previously (p. 71).

Thus, the following are statutorily exempted from it: (*a*) women, (*b*) men who have not yet reached full maturity, (*c*) old men, (*d*) the sick and the crippled, (*e*) the destitute, (*f*) priests and monks, and (*g*) all men who choose to render military service.

Limits of Obedience

After this digression into the problems of *jihād* and military service, let us return to our consideration of the duties incumbent upon the citizens of an Islamic state, and especially to the question of allegiance.

So long as the state conforms in its principles and methods to the demands of the *sharīʿah*, a Muslim citizen's duty of obedience to the government is a religious obligation. In the words of the Prophet,

من خلع يداً من طاعة لقى الله يوم القيامة ولا حجة له، ومن مات وليس فى عنقه بيعة مات ميتة جاهلية.

> He who withdraws his hand from obedience [to the *amīr*] will have nothing in his favor when he meets God on the Day of Resurrection; and he who dies without having considered himself bound by a pledge of allegiance [literally, "while there is no pledge of allegiance on his neck"] has died the death of the Time of Ignorance [i.e., as an unbeliever].[16]

In accordance with the principle of Muslim unity so strongly emphasized in Qur'ān and Sunnah, any attempt to disrupt that unity must be regarded as a crime of the highest order—in fact, as high treason—and must be punished severely. Consequently, the Prophet commanded:

أيما رجل خرج يفرق بين أمتى فاضربوا عنقه. من أتاكم وأمركم جميع على رجل واحد يريد أن يشق عصاكم أو يفرق جماعتكم فاقتلوه.

"Whoever it be that goes forth to divide my community, smite his neck."[17] "If, while you are united under one man's leadership,

[16] Muslim, on the authority of Ibn ʿUmar.
[17] An-Nasā'ī, on the authority of Usāmah ibn Sharīk.

anyone tries to break your strength or to disrupt your unity, kill him."[18]

However, a Muslim's duty of allegiance to the government, represented by the person of the *amīr*, is not unconditional. As has been laid down by the highest authority—the Prophet himself—the first condition of allegiance is a person's individual ability to fulfill the duties arising therefrom. Thus, ʿAbd Allāh ibn ʿUmar reports:

كنا إذا بايعنا رسول الله (صلعم) على السمع والطاعة يقول لنا : " فيما استطعتم ."

"Whenever we gave our pledge to the Apostle of God to hear and to obey, he used to say to us, 'Insofar as you are able to do so.'"[19] We may safely presume that the Prophet never imposed on his followers any duty that went beyond their capabilities; but, as the Law-Giver of his community, he undoubtedly wanted to make it known that the duty of "hearing and obeying" any earthly authority whatever is subject to certain limitations. Physical inability due to circumstances beyond a citizen's control could be one of them; moral inability, another. It was to the latter limitation that the Prophet referred when he said:

لا طاعة فى معصية ، إنما الطاعة فى المعروف .

"No obedience is due in sinful matters: behold, obedience is due only in the way of righteousness [*fi 'l-maʿrūf*]."[20] In other versions of this Tradition, the Prophet is reported to have used the expressions,

لا طاعة لمن لم يطع الله

"No obedience is due to him who does not obey God,"[21] and

لا طاعة لمن عصى الله تعالى

"No obedience is due to him who rebels against God."[22]

[18] Muslim, on the authority of ʿArfajah.
[19] Al-Bukhārī and Muslim, on the authority of Ibn ʿUmar.
[20] *Ibid.*, on the authority of ʿAlī.
[21] Aḥmad ibn Ḥanbal, on the authority of Muʿādh ibn Jabal.
[22] *Ibid.*, on the authority of ʿUbādah ibn aṣ-Ṣāmit.

All this naturally presupposes the citizens' right and duty to watch over the activities of the government and to criticize its administrative and legislative policy whenever there is reason to suppose that matters are wrongly handled. There are many verses in the Qur'ān and many sayings of the Prophet to the effect that to raise one's voice against manifest wrong is one of the foremost duties of a Muslim, and particularly so when the wrongdoer is the established authority. Thus, the Apostle of God said:

أفضل الجهاد من قال كلمة الحق عند سلطان جائر

"The highest kind of *jihād* is to speak up for truth in the face of a government [*sulṭān*] that deviates from the right path."[23] And:

من رأى منكم منكراً فليغيره بيده ، فإن لم يستطع فبلسانه ، فإن لم يستطع فبقلبه – وذلك أضعف الايمان .

"If any of you sees something evil, he should set it right by his hand; if he is unable to do so, then by his tongue; and if he is unable to do even that, then within his heart—but this is the weakest form of faith."[24] In other words, the Prophet considered the removal of wrong by action as the highest form of faith; and this principle ought to apply to the citizens' attitude towards an unjust government.

But do the words of the Prophet imply the citizens' right to rise in rebellion against the government whenever it contravenes any of the *sharʿī* laws? Obviously not; for the Prophet has ordained that

من بايع إماماً فأعطاه صفقة يده وثمرة قلبه فليطعه إن استطاع

"He who has pledged allegiance to a leader [*imām*], giving him his hand and the fruit of his heart, shall obey him if [or: "as long

[23] Abū Dā'ūd, At-Tirmidhī, and Ibn Mājah, on the authority of Abū Saʿīd al-Khudrī.

[24] Muslim, on the authority of Abū Saʿīd al-Khudrī.

as"] he can"[25]—that is to say, so long as the *imām* upholds the values of Islam in general and does not deliberately forsake its aims. An occasional lapse on his part does not entitle the citizens —at least so long as the majority of the community has not pronounced itself against him—to revolt against his government. Thus, the Prophet said:

من رأى من أميره شيئاً فكره فليصبر ، فإنه ليس أحد يفارق الجماعة فيموت إلا مات ميتة جاهلية .

> If anyone sees in his *amīr* something that displeases him, let him [nevertheless] remain patient; for, behold, he who separates himself from the united community by even so much as a handspan and dies thereupon, has died the death of the Time of Ignorance.[26]

How long, then, and to what extent shall the citizens exercise patience with an unjust government? An answer to this question is forthcoming from several authentic Traditions and particularly from the following two, which must be read together:

قال رسول الله (صلعم) : "خيار أئمتكم الذين تحبونهم ويحبونكم وتصلون عليهم ويصلون عليكم ، وشرار أئمتكم الذين تبغضونهم ويبغضونكم وتلعنونهم ويلعنونكم." قلنا : "يا رسول الله ! أفلا ننابذهم عند ذلك؟" قال : "لا ما أقاموا فيكم الصلوة ، لا ما أقاموا فيكم الصلوة !"

> The Apostle of God said: "The best of your leaders are those whom you love and who love you, those upon whom you invoke blessings and who invoke blessings upon you; the worst of your leaders are those whom you hate and who hate you, those whom you curse and who curse you." We [i.e., the Companions present] asked: "O Apostle of God! Should we not overthrow them, if such is the case?" He replied: "No, so long as they uphold prayer among you; no, so long as they uphold prayer among you!"[27]

[25] Muslim, on the authority of ʿAbd Allāh ibn ʿAmr.
[26] Al-Bukhārī and Muslim, on the authority of ʿAbd Allāh ibn ʿAbbās.
[27] Muslim, on the authority of ʿAwf ibn Mālik al-Ashjaʿī.

It is obvious that, in this context, the "upholding of prayer" has a far wider meaning than the mere holding of congregational prayers: it denotes—as it does at the beginning of the second chapter of the Qur'ān[28]—a positive upholding of the Faith.

The other Tradition, narrated by the Companion 'Ubādah ibn aṣ-Ṣāmit, runs as follows:

دعانا النبى (صلعم) فبايعناه ، فقال فيما أخذ علينا أن بايعنا على السمع والطاعة
فى منشطنا ومكرهنا وعسرنا ويسرنا وأثرة علينـا وأن لا ننازع الأمـر أهلـه "إلا أن
تروا كفراً بواحاً عندكم من الله فيه .برهان ."

> The Prophet called us, and we pledged our allegiance to him. He imposed on us the duty to hear and obey in whatever pleases and displeases us, in hardship as well as in ease, whatever our personal preference, and [impressed on us] that we should not withdraw authority from those who have been entrusted with it, "unless you see an obvious infidelity [*kufr*] for which you have a clear proof from [the Book of] God."[29]

From the context of all the Traditions relating to this point, four principles are self-evident: (1) so long as the *amīr* represents the legally established government, all citizens owe him their allegiance, however much one or another of them may dislike his person and, on occasion, even his administrative acts; (2) if the government issues laws or regulations which involve the commission of a sin in the strict *shar'ī* sense, the duty of obedience ceases to be operative with regard to these laws or regulations; (3) if the government sets itself openly and deliberately against the *naṣṣ* ordinances of the Qur'ān, it may be deemed to have become guilty of infidelity, whereupon authority should be withdrawn from it; and (4) this withdrawal of authority must never be brought about by armed rebellion on the part of a minority within the community —for the Prophet has warned,

من حمل علينا السلاح فليس منا

[28] Qur'ān 2:3.

[29] Al-Bukhārī, on the authority of 'Ubādah ibn aṣ-Ṣāmit. An almost identical Tradition has been quoted by Muslim as well.

"He who raises arms against us ceases to be one of us [i.e., ceases to belong to the Muslim community]."[30] And,

من سلّ علينا السيف فليس منا

"He who unsheaths his sword against us ceases to be one of us."[31]

It is, therefore, evident that the Muslims have been authorized by the Prophet to disobey the orders of the government which are contrary to the *sharī'ah*, and to depose the government if its behavior amounts to flagrant infidelity. However, in consonance with the principle of communal unity insisted upon so frequently by Qur'ān and Sunnah, it cannot possibly be left to the discretion of individual citizens to decide at what point obedience to the *amīr* ceases to be a religious and civic duty: decisions of this kind can be taken only by the community as a whole or by its properly appointed representatives. One might suppose that the proper authority in such an event would be the *majlis ash-shūrā*; but against this stands our finding that conflicts of opinion between the *majlis* and the *amīr* might lead to insoluble deadlocks unless recourse is taken to impartial arbitration, that is, to a supreme tribunal. In the preceding chapter I have mentioned that it would be the duty of this tribunal to invalidate any law or administrative regulation which contravenes the *sharī'ah*; similarly, it would fall within the purview of the tribunal to order the holding of a popular referendum on the question of the *amīr*'s deposition from office if an impeachment is preferred against him to the effect that he governs in deliberate opposition to Islamic Law. If, by means of such a referendum, the majority of the community pronounce themselves against the *amīr*, he must be regarded as having been legally deposed, whereupon the people's pledge of allegiance to him ceases to be effective.

Thus, the citizens' duty to watch over the activities of the government, and their right to criticize it and, in the last resort,

[30] Al-Bukhārī and Muslim, on the authority of 'Abd Allāh ibn 'Umar and Abū Hurayrah.

[31] Muslim, on the authority of Salamah ibn al-Akwa'.

to depose it, should on no account be confused with a (non-existent) right to rebellion by an individual or a group of individuals. It is only by an open verdict of the majority within the community that an established Muslim government may be removed from power—by peaceful means if possible, and by force if necessary.

Freedom of Opinion

However, it is not only on the question of whether a government is to be deposed (a question which probably would arise only on rare occasions) that a Muslim citizen is obliged to exert his critical faculties and to summon his moral courage to stand up for right and justice: for, according to the Qur'ān, he is duty-bound to combat evil wherever he encounters it, and to strive for justice whenever people disregard it. The Prophet said:

والذى نفسى بيده ! لتأمرن بالمعروف وتنهون عن المنكر أو ليوشكن الله أن يبعث عليكم عذاباً من عنده ، ثم لتدعنه ولا يستجاب لكم.

"By Him in Whose hand I repose! You must enjoin right and forbid wrong, or else God will certainly send down chastisement upon you; then you will call to Him, but He will not respond to you."[32]

God's punishment may not always be limited to the individuals who are remiss in this respect: it may well, as the Prophet has pointed out, affect the destinies of the entire community:

كلا والله ! لتأمرن بالمعروف ولتنهون عن المنكر ولتأخذن على يدى الظالم ولتأطرنه على الحق أطراً ولتقصرنه على الحق قصراً أو ليضربن الله قلوب بعضكم على بعض.

"Nay, by God, you must enjoin right and forbid wrong, and you must stay the hand of the wrongdoer, bend him to conformity with justice [*al-ḥaqq*] and force him to do justice—or else God will set the hearts of you all against one another."[33] And:

إذا رأوا الظالم فلم يأخذوا على يديه أوشك أن يعمهم الله بعقابه

"If people see a wrongdoer but do not stay his hand, it is most

[32] At-Tirmidhī, on the authority of Ḥudhayfah.
[33] Abū Dā'ūd, on the authority of 'Abd Allāh ibn Mas'ūd.

likely that God will encompass them all with His punishment."[34] In another version of the same Tradition, the Prophet is reported to have said:

ما من قوم يعمل فيهم بالمعاصى ثم يقدرون على أن يغيروا ثم لا يغيرون إلا يوشك أن يعمهم الله بعقاب

"A community in the midst of which sins are being committed which could be, but are not, corrected by it is most likely to be encompassed in its entirety by God's punishment."[35] Thus, it is in the interests of the whole community that its members strive for an improvement of moral and social conditions wherever and whenever possible: for,

إن الله لا يغير ما بقوم حتى يغيروا ما بأنفسهم

"Behold, God does not change a people's circumstances unless they bring about a change in their inner selves."[36] It is to be borne in mind that this law of interdependence between a people's moral attitude and its outward circumstances acts both ways: while an improvement in a nation's moral structure is bound, in the long run, to lead to greater material well-being and political power, moral decay must as unavoidably result in social, economic, and political decay.

Any positive change—that is, a change in the direction of moral and social improvement—can come about only if the community becomes aware of its *necessity*: consequently, it is the duty of every thinking Muslim to subject his social environment to continuous, searching criticism, and to give voice to this criticism for the common good. The Apostle of God said:

لا حسد إلا فى إثنين : رجل آته الله مالاً فسلطه على هلكته فى الحق ، ورجل آته الله الحكمة فهو يقضى بها ويعلمها .

Only two [kinds of men] may rightly be envied: a man whom

[34] Abū Dā'ūd, on the authority of Abū Bakr.
[35] *Ibid.*, on the authority of Abū Bakr.
[36] Qur'ān 13:11.

> God has given wealth and thereupon endowed him with the strength to give it away in the cause of justice; and a man whom God has given wisdom and who acts in its spirit and imparts it [to others].[37]

Thus, the duty of criticism and advice—so necessary for a healthy growth of civic consciousness in the Islamic sense—does not exhaust all the ideological obligations of the individual citizen toward the community. We have seen that a truly Islamic life presupposes and demands unceasing *ijtihād* in all matters not laid down in terms of law in the incontrovertible, self-evident *naṣṣ* ordinances of Qur'ān and Sunnah; and this liberty of *ijtihād* becomes a moral and social duty whenever matters of communal concern are under discussion. In other words, the intellectual leaders of the community are morally bound to bring forward whatever new ideas they may have relating to communal progress, and to advocate such ideas in public; and for this reason the right to a free expression of one's opinions in speech and in writing is one of the fundamental rights of the citizen of an Islamic state. It must, of course, be understood that such freedom of opinion and of its expression (which naturally includes the freedom of the press) must not be used for incitement against the Law of Islam or sedition against the established government, and must not be allowed to offend against common decency.

The Protection of Citizens

We have seen that the Muslim is not only legally but also morally bound always to subordinate his personal interests to the interests of the Islamic state as a whole, and this in pursuance of the principle that such a state is "God's vice-gerent on earth." It is obvious, however, that the state's religious claim to the citizen's allegiance must not be one-sided: that is to say, the relationship between state and citizen cannot be restricted to obligations imposed on the citizen, or even to certain freedoms accorded to him by the state—as, for instance, the freedom of opinion and of its

[37] Al-Bukhārī and Muslim, on the authority of Ibn Mas'ūd.

expression, the right of voting a government into office and of removing it from office—but must also be reflected in certain well-defined, positive obligations of the state with regard to its citizens.

A counterpart of the Muslim citizens' duty to render military service is the state's duty to afford them protection against external and internal enemies. Similarly, the individual citizen's obligation to respect and honor the legally established government must find its counterpart in the government's duty to extend its protection to the private lives of the citizens. In accordance with the general tenets of Islam, the Prophet declared in his famous sermon at ʿArafāt, on the occasion of his Farewell Pilgrimage:

إن دماءكم وأموالكم حرام عليكم كحرمة يومكم هذا

"Behold, your lives and your possessions shall be as inviolable among you as the sacred inviolability of this very day [of Pilgrimage]."[38] And on another occasion he said:

كل المسلم على المسلم حرام دمه وماله وعرضه

"The blood, property and honour of a Muslim must be sacred [*ḥarām*] to every [other] Muslim."[39] This, taken together with many other similar injunctions in Qurʾān and Sunnah, calls for an incorporation in the constitution of an Islamic state of a clause to the effect that the lives, persons, and possessions of the citizens are inviolable, and that none shall be deprived of his life, freedom, or property, except by due process of law.

The protection which the state must grant to the citizens is not limited to the tangible factors of their existence, such as their persons and possessions, but must extend to their dignity and honor and the privacy of their homes as well. The Qurʾān says:

ويل لكل همزة لمزة ! يا أيها الذين آمنوا اجتنبوا كثيراً من الظن إن بعض الظن إثم ، ولا تجسسوا ولا يغتب بعضكم بعضا .

[38] Muslim, on the authority of Jābir ibn ʿAbd Allāh.
[39] *Ibid.*, on the authority of Abū Hurayrah.

"Woe to every slandering defamer!"[40] "O you who believe! Avoid suspicion as much as you can, for, behold, suspicion is sometimes a sin; and do not spy upon one another, and do not defame one another behind your backs."[41] It was in this spirit that the Prophet admonished his followers:

إياكم والظن ، فإن الظن أكذب الحديث ، ولا تجسسوا ولا تحسسوا . لا تؤذوا المسلمين ولا تعيروا ولا تتبعوا عوراتهم ، فإنه من يتبع عورة أخيه المسلم يتبع الله عورته .

> Beware of suspicion, for suspicion [may be based on] a most untrue information; and do not spy upon one another, and do not try to bare each other's hidden failings.[42] Do not harm other Muslims, do not impute evil to them, and do not try to uncover their nakedness: for, behold, if anyone tries to uncover the nakedness of his brother Muslim, God will uncover his own nakedness.[43]

And, finally,

إن الأمير إذا ابتغى الريبة فى الناس أفسدهم

"If the *amīr* falls into suspecting the people, he causes them to become dishonest."[44]

All these Traditions, read in conjunction with the Qur'ān verse,

يا أيها الذين آمنوا لا تدخلوا بيوتاً غير بيوتكم حتى تستأنسوا وتسلموا على أهلها

"O you who believe! Do not enter houses other than your own unless you have obtained permission and saluted their inmates,"[45] call for a constitutional enactment which would guarantee the inviolability of a citizen's home, private life, and honor, and would prohibit the government from indulging in activities that might

[40] Qur'ān 104:1.
[41] *Ibid.*, 49:12.
[42] Mālik ibn Anas, on the authority of Abū Hurayrah. Almost identical versions of this Tradition have also been quoted by Al-Bukhārī, Muslim, and Abū Dā'ūd.
[43] At-Tirmidhī, on the authority of 'Abd Allāh ibn 'Umar.
[44] Abū Dā'ūd, on the authority of Abū Umāmah.
[45] Qur'ān 24:27.

run counter to this fundamental guarantee. Thus, subjection of citizens, other than those previously convicted of felony, to secret police supervision would be entirely out of bounds in a truly Islamic state; arrest on mere suspicion would be a breach of constitutional law; and imprisonment or internment without previous trial and conviction by a duly established court of law would clearly contravene the principle of the inviolability of the human person laid down so unequivocally in Qur'ān and Sunnah.

Free and Compulsory Education

A logical corollary of the citizen's duty to watch scrupulously over the activities of the government is, as already mentioned, the freedom of opinion and of its expression guaranteed by Islam to all mature members of the community. But the duty and the right to express one's opinion freely may be meaningless—and on occasion even injurious to the best interests of the society—if those opinions are not based on sound thought, which, in its turn, presupposes the possession of sound knowledge. Consequently, it is the citizens' right and the government's duty to have a system of education which would make knowledge freely accessible to every man and woman in the state. Both Qur'ān and Sunnah are full of injunctions relating to the acquisition of knowledge, and the Prophet stressed its supreme value on innumerable occasions, as, for instance:

من سلك طريقاً يلتمس فيه علماً سهل الله له به طريقاً الى الجنة. إن فضل العالم على العابد كفضل القمر ليلة البدر على سائر الكواكب.

"If anybody goes on his way in search of knowledge, God will thereby make easy for him the way to Paradise."[46] "The superiority of the learned man over a [mere] worshipper is like the superiority of the moon when it is full over all the stars."[47] And he went even further than that:

فضل العالم على العابد كفضلي على أدناكم

[46] Muslim, on the authority of Abū Hurayrah.

[47] At-Tirmidhī, Abū Dā'ūd, and Aḥmad ibn Ḥanbal, on the authority of Abū 'd-Dardā'.

"The superiority of the learned man over a [mere] worshipper is like my superiority over the least of you."[48] And, finally:

طلب العلم فريضة على كل مسلم ومسلمة

"Search for knowledge is a sacred duty [*farīḍah*] imposed on every Muslim man and woman."[49]

It follows, therefore, that a state which owes its justification to the call of Islam and aims at establishing the Law of Islam as the law of the land must make education not only accessible but also compulsory for every Muslim man and woman; and because it is one of the basic tenets of such a state to make all the facilities of life available to its non-Muslim citizens as well, education must be free and compulsory for all citizens, regardless of religion.

Economic Security

Finally, in order to justify in the fullest measure its claim to the citizens' allegiance, the state must assume active responsibility for their material welfare: in other words, it falls within the responsibility of the state to provide its citizens with such economic facilities as are necessary for the maintenance of human happiness and dignity. Nothing could illustrate this principle better than the following saying of the Apostle of God:

ألا كلكم راع وكلكم مسئول عن رعيته ؛ فالإمام الذى على الناس راع وهو مسئول عن رعيته ، والرجل راع على أهل بيته وهو مسئول عن رعيته ، والمرأة راعية على أهل بيت زوجها وولده وهى مسئولة عنهم ، وعبد الرجل راع على مال سيده وهو مسئول عنه ؛ ألا فكلكم راع وكلكم مسئول عن رعيته .

> Behold, every one of you is a shepherd; and every one is responsible for his flock. Thus, the *imām* [i.e., the government] that has been placed over the people is a shepherd, and is responsible for his flock; and every man is a shepherd over his family, and is responsible for his flock; and the woman is a shepherdess over her husband's household and his children,

48 At-Tirmidhī, on the authority of Abū Umāmah al-Bāhilī.
49 Ibn Mājah, on the authority of Anas.

> and is responsible for them; and the servant is a shepherd over his master's property, and is responsible for it. Behold, every one of you is a shepherd, and every one is responsible for his flock.[50]

The reader will not have failed to observe that in this Tradition the government's responsibility toward the citizens has been put on a par with a father's or a mother's responsibility toward their children. Just as the father is a "shepherd"—that is, a guardian—morally and legally bound to ensure the maintenance and well-being of his family, the government is morally and legally bound to ensure the economic well-being of the citizens whose affairs it administers, and to see to it that no person's standard of living falls below an equitable level. For, although Islam has made it clear that human life cannot be expressed in terms of physical existence alone—the ultimate values of life being spiritual in nature—the Muslims are not entitled to look upon spiritual truths and values as something that could be divorced from the physical factors of human existence. In short, Islam demands a society that is righteous not only in its moral outlook, but in its deeds as well; a society that provides not only for the spiritual needs of its members, but for their bodily needs as well. It follows, therefore, that a state, in order to be truly Islamic, must arrange the affairs of the community in such a way that every individual, man and woman, shall enjoy that minimum of material well-being without which there can be no human dignity, no real freedom and, in the last resort, no spiritual progress. This, of course, does not mean that the state should, or ever could, ensure easy and carefree living to its citizens: it only means that in an Islamic state there shall be no soul-grinding poverty side by side with affluence; secondly, that all the resources of the state must be harnessed to the task of providing adequate means of livelihood for all its citizens; and, thirdly, that all the opportunities in this respect should be open to all citizens equally, and that no person should enjoy a high standard of living at the expense of others.

[50] Al-Bukhārī and Muslim, on the authority of ʿAbd Allāh ibn ʿUmar.

The Prophet said:

المؤمن للمؤمن كالبنيان يشد بعضه بعضا

"The Faithful are to one another like [parts of] a building—each part strengthening the others."[51] Thus, mutual coöperation in all phases of life is a fundamental requirement of Islam; and no state can be called Islamic unless it guides that coöperation by legislative means, and thereby enables its citizens to live up to the demands of Islam as enunciated by the Apostle of God:

لا تدخلون الجنة حتى تؤمنوا ، ولا تؤمنوا حتى تحابوا . أرحموا من فى الأرض يرحمكم من فى السماء. لا يرحم الله من لا يرحم الناس .

> You shall not enter Paradise until you have faith; and you cannot attain to faith until you love one another.[52] Have compassion on those who are on earth, and He Who is in heaven will have compassion on you.[53] God will show no compassion to him who has no compassion toward all human beings.[54]

And, more specifically:

أيما مسلم كسا مسلماً ثوباً على عرى كساه الله من خضر الجنة ، وأيما مسلم أطعم مسلماً على جوع أطعمه الله من ثمار الجنة ، وأيما مسلم سقى مسلماً على ضماء سقاه الله من الرحيق المختوم .

> If a Muslim clothes another Muslim in his nudity, God will clothe him with the green freshness of Paradise; and if a Muslim feeds a Muslim who is hungry, God will give him to eat of the fruits of Paradise; and if a Muslim gives a drink to a thirsty Muslim, God will let him drink from the fountain of Paradise.[55]

And, finally:

[51] Al-Bukhārī and Muslim, on the authority of Abū Mūsā.
[52] Muslim, on the authority of Abū Hurayrah.
[53] At-Tirmidhī and Abū Dā'ūd, on the authority of ʿAbd Allāh ibn ʿAmr.
[54] Al-Bukhārī and Muslim, on the authority of Jarīr ibn ʿAbd Allāh.
[55] At-Tirmidhī and Abū Dā'ūd, on the authority of Abū Saʿīd.

ليس المؤمن بالذى يشبع وجاره جائع الى جنبه

"He is not a Faithful who eats his fill while his neighbor remains hungry by his side."[56]

Lest his followers think that he merely admonished them to practice charity in their individual capacities, the Prophet often stressed the social aspect of mutual help and coöperation:

المؤمنون كرجل واحد : إن اشتكى عينه اشتكى كله ، وإن اشتكى رأسه اشتكى كله . ترى المؤمنين فى تراحمهم وتوادهم وتعاطفهم كمثل الجسد : إذا اشتكى عضواً تداعى له سائر الجسد بالسهو والحمى .

> The Faithful are like one man: if his eye suffers, his whole body suffers; and if his head suffers, his whole body suffers.[57] You will recognize the Faithful by their mutual compassion, love and sympathy. They are like one body: if one of its parts is ill, the whole body suffers from sleeplessness and fever.[58]

This, then, is the deepest sociological lesson of Islam: there can be no happiness and strength in a society that permits some of its members to suffer undeserved want while others have more than they need. If the whole society suffers privations owing to extraordinary circumstances (as, for instance, happened to the Muslim community in the early days of Islam), such privations may become the source of spiritual strength and, through it, of future greatness. But if the available resources of a community are so unevenly distributed that certain groups within it live in affluence while the majority of the people are forced to use up all their energies in search of their daily bread, poverty becomes the most dangerous enemy of spiritual progress, and occasionally drives whole communities away from God-consciousness and into the arms of soul-destroying materialism. It is undoubtedly this that the Prophet had in mind when he uttered the warning words:

كاد الفقر أن يكون كفراً

[56] Al-Bayhaqī, on the authority of Ibn ʿAbbās.
[57] Muslim, on the authority of Nuʿmān ibn Bashīr.
[58] Al-Bukhārī and Muslim, on the authority of Nuʿmān ibn Bashīr.

"Poverty may sometimes turn into unbelief [*kufr*]."[59]

Poverty in the midst of plenty is a negation of the very principle of brotherhood by which Islam stands and falls. The Prophet said:

والذى نفسى بيده ! لا يؤمن عبد حتى يحب لأخيه ما يحب لنفسه .

"By Him in Whose hand I repose! No one has real faith unless he desires for his brother that which he desires for himself."[60] Consequently, the Islamic state must see to it that equity prevails within the community, and that every citizen—man, woman and child—shall have enough to eat and to wear, shall be succored in case of illness, and have a decent home in which to live. In pursuance of this aim, the constitution of the country must contain a provision to the effect that every citizen has a right to (*a*) productive and remunerative work while of working age and in good health, (*b*) training—at the expense of the state, if necessary—for such productive work, (*c*) free and efficient health services in case of illness, and (*d*) a provision by the state of adequate nourishment, clothing and shelter in cases of disability resulting from illness, widowhood, unemployment due to circumstances beyond individual control, old age, or under-age.

Such a constitutional enactment would presuppose the creation of a nationwide social insurance scheme, to be financed by means of a comprehensive taxation of wealth in accordance with the Prophet's injunction that

تؤخذ من أغنيائهم فترد على فقرائهم

"it shall be taken from the rich among them and turned over to the poor among them"[61]—both through *zakāt* and through additional taxes on property and revenue; for, in the words of the Prophet,

إن فى المال حق سواء الزكوة

"There is indeed a duty [*ḥaqq*] on property apart from *zakāt*."[62]

59 As-Suyūṭī, *Al-Jāmi' aṣ-ṣaghīr*.
60 Al-Bukhārī and Muslim, on the authority of Anas.
61 *Ibid.*, on the authority of 'Abd Allāh ibn 'Abbās.
62 At-Tirmidhī and Ibn Mājah, on the authority of Fāṭimah bint Qays.

If some readers suppose that the idea of such a social insurance scheme is an invention of the twentieth century, I would remind them of the fact that it was in full swing many centuries before its present name was coined, and even before the need for it became apparent under the impact of modern industrial civilization: namely, in the Islamic Commonwealth at the time of the Right-Guided Caliphs. It was ʿUmar the Great who, in the year 20 A.H., inaugurated a special government department, called *dīwān*, for the purpose of holding a census of the population at regular intervals. On the basis of this census, annual state pensions were fixed for (*a*) widows and orphans, (*b*) all persons who had been in the forefront of the struggle for Islam during the lifetime of the Prophet, beginning with his widows, the survivors of the Battle of Badr, the early *muhājirs*, and so forth, and (*c*) all disabled, sick, and old persons. The minimum pension payable under this scheme amounted to two hundred and fifty *dirhams* annually. In time, a regular allowance, payable to their parents or guardians, was settled even on children (on the principle that they were unable to fend for themselves) from the moment of their birth to the time when they would reach maturity; and during the last year of his life, ʿUmar said more than once: "If God grants me life, I shall see to it that even the lonely shepherd in the mountains of Ṣanʿā' shall have his share in the wealth of the community."[63] With his characteristic grasp of practical issues, ʿUmar even went so far as to make experiments with a group of thirty people with a view to finding out the minimum amount of food an average person needed to maintain full health and vigor; and on the conclusion of these experiments he ordained that every man and woman in the country should receive from the government storehouses (in addition to the monetary pension of which he or she might be a recipient) a monthly allowance of wheat sufficient for two square meals a day.[64] However, before he could complete his grand scheme of social insurance, ʿUmar fell victim to a murderer's dagger, and his

[63] Ibn Saʿd, Vol. III/1, pp. 213-217.
[64] *Ibid.*, pp. 219-220.

successors had neither the vision nor the administrative ability to continue his unfinished work.

Here, as at so many other points of Islamic history, a glorious beginning was allowed to lapse into oblivion, to the detriment of Islam and of the social development of its followers. Is it not our duty, with thirteen centuries of historical experience at our disposal, to rectify that shameful negligence and to bring 'Umar's work to completion?

The Apostle of God said:

إن الله تعالى يقول يوم القيامة : "يا ابن آدم ! مرضت فلم تعدنى ." قال : "يا رب ، كيف أعودك وأنت رب العالمن ؟" قال : " أما علمت أن عبدى فلان مرض فلم تعده ؟ أما علمت أنك لو عدته لوجدتنى عنده ؟ يا ابن آدم ! استطعمتك فلم تطعمنى ." قال : "يا رب ، كيف أطعمك وأنت رب العالمين ؟" قال : "أما علمت أنه استطعمك عبدى فلان فلم تطعمه ؟ أما علمت أنك لو أطعمته لوجدت ذلك عندى ؟ يا ابن آدم ! استسقيتك فلم تسقنى ." قال : "يا رب ، كيف أسقيك وأنت رب العالمين ؟" قال : "أستسقاك عبدى فلان فلم تسقه ، أما علمت أنك لو سقيته وجدت ذلك عندى ؟"

> Behold, God will say on the Day of Resurrection: "O son of Adam! I was ill, and you did not succor Me." Man will exclaim: "O Lord, how could I have succored Thee, the Lord of all the worlds?" And God will reply: "Did you not know that such and such of My servants was ill, and you did not succor him? Did you not know that if you had done so, you would indeed have found Me with him? O son of Adam! I asked you for food, but you did not feed Me."—"O Lord, how could I have fed Thee, the Lord of all the worlds?" Whereupon God will say: "Did you not know that such and such of My servants asked you for food, and you did not feed him? Did you not know that if you had done so, you would indeed have found it [again] with Me? O son of Adam! I asked you for a drink, but you did not give me to drink." Man will say thereupon: "How could I have given Thee, the Lord of all the worlds, to drink?" But God will reply: "Such and such of My servants asked you for a drink, but you did not

give it to him. Did you not know that if you had given him to drink, you would have found it [again] with Me?"[65]

[65] Muslim, on the authority of Abū Hurayrah.

Chapter VI

CONCLUSION

The Obstacles in Our Way

Here ends our discussion of the fundamental *sharʿī* principles which must find their expression in the constitution of a state that is to be Islamic not only in name but also in fact.

I have not attempted to set forth in this book anything like a "blueprint" for the constitution of a state. I have merely tried to bring out some of the self-evident injunctions of Islam relevant to the problem of state and government, to discuss the modalities of their application to present-day needs, and to draw attention to the legal provisions which must under all circumstances be included in a constitution that claims to be Islamic. Within the narrow confines of this task, I have endeavored to show that Islam offers us a definite, clear-cut outline of a political law of its own, leaving it to the *ijtihād* of the time concerned to elaborate the details.

Needless to say, a mere discussion of the forms and procedures that ought to underlie the organization of an Islamic state cannot do full justice to the entire scheme of Islam. For Islam is much more than a program of political action: it is a system of beliefs and morals, a social doctrine, and a call to righteousness in all individual and communal concerns; it is a complete, self-contained ideology which regards all aspects of our existence—moral and physical, spiritual and intellectual, personal and communal—as parts of the indivisible whole which we call "human life." But precisely *because* the ideology of Islam is so complete and so self-contained, its adherents cannot live a truly Islamic life merely by holding Islamic beliefs. They must do far more than that. If Islam is not to remain an empty word, they must also coördinate their outward social behavior with the beliefs they profess. Such a coördination of attitude and endeavor is impossible unless the whole community is subject to the socioeconomic laws of Islam: and so it is only within the framework of an independent ideological state built on the principles of Islam and endowed with all the machinery of government, legislation, and law-enforcement that the ideals of Islam can be brought to practical fruition.

In a world like ours, which for the most part is governed by concepts of nationalism along racial or, at best, along purely cultural lines, the concept of an Islamic state is so far removed from what the rest of the world regards as "modern" and desirable, that the advocacy of a religious ideology as the basis of state-organization is bound to encounter formidable opposition. Most people of our time have grown accustomed to accepting racial affinities and historical traditions as the only legitimate premises of nationhood: whereas we Muslims, on the other hand, regard an ideological community—a community of people having a definite outlook on life and a definite scale of moral values in common—as the highest form of nationhood to which man can aspire. We make this claim not only because we are convinced that our particular ideology, Islam, is a Law decreed by God Himself, but also because our reason tells us that a community based on *ideas* held in common is a far more advanced manifestation of human life than a community resulting from race or language or geographical location.

We should not underestimate the difficulties that will confront us should we decide to give to our polity the contents and forms demanded by Islam. For one thing, it is no easy task to achieve a truly Islamic polity after the centuries of debasement and slavery which have sapped the strength of the Muslim community and undermined its social morale. During the period of their political decay, the Muslims have lost a good deal of their cultural self-confidence as well, and many of them find it difficult today to avoid thinking in Western terms of "state" and "nation" and to think in Islamic terms instead. They blindly follow Western patterns of thought in the naïve belief that everything which comes from the West must be more "up-to-date" than anything which they, the

Muslims, could produce out of themselves; and this conviction leads them to an irresponsible application of Western political concepts to all that happens in their own society. On the other hand, many conservative Muslims who, in word and deed, insist on the maintenance of all traditional forms and, consequently, oppose the Westernization of their community, base their opposition not so much on the real values of Islam as on the social conventions evolved in the centuries of our decadence. Their minds seem to work on the assumption that Islam and the conventions of Muslim society are one and the same thing (which every thinking person knows is an utterly false assumption) and that, therefore, everything that implies a departure from the conventions evolved in the course of our history—both with regard to our social habits and our approach to the problem of state and government—goes against Islam; and that, therefore, it would be the duty of an Islamic state to give permanence and legal sanction to all the social forms in which we have hitherto been living. In other words, these conservative elements within our society seem to take it for granted that the survival of Islam depends on the maintenance of the very conditions which, because of their sterile rigidity, now make it impossible for Muslims to live in accordance with the true tenets of Islam. This, the reader will admit, is very poor logic; but however absurd these assumptions may be, they nevertheless provide the basis on which the minds of our conservative critics operate. Their unwillingness to concede the necessity of *any* change in our social concepts and habits drives countless Muslim men and women to a helpless imitation of the West; and their insistence that a modern Islamic state would have to be an exact replica of the "historic precedents" of our past is apt to bring the very idea of the Islamic state into discredit and ridicule.

Apart from the difficulties arising from our own cultural decadence and the centuries-old stagnation of Muslim thought, any attempt to reorganize our countries on truly Islamic lines invariably arouses apprehensions in the non-Muslim world and causes it to place all manner of obstructions, direct and indirect, in our way toward this ideal. Ever since the Crusades, Islam has been misrepresented in the West, and a deep distrust—almost hatred—of all Islamic propositions has become part and parcel of the Western cultural heritage. The Westerners see in the tenets of Islam not only a denial of many of the fundamental beliefs of their own religion but also a political threat. Under the influence of their historical memories, of the centuries of passionate warfare between the Muslim world and Europe, they attribute to Islam—quite unjustifiably—an inherent hostility toward all non-Muslims; and so they fear that a revival of the Islamic spirit, as manifested in the idea of the Islamic state, might revive the slumbering strength of the Muslims and drive them to new aggressive adventures in the direction of the West. To counteract such a possible tendency, the Westerners are doing their utmost to prevent a resurgence of political power in Muslim countries and a restoration of Islam to its erstwhile dominant position in Muslim social and intellectual life. Their means of combat are not merely political; they are cultural as well. Through the instrumentality of Western schools and of Western-orientated methods of education in the Muslim world, the distrust of Islam as a social doctrine is being systematically planted in the minds of the younger generation of Muslim men and women; and the principal weapon in this campaign to discredit Islam is being supplied, unconsciously, by the reactionary elements within our own society. By insisting that the political forms and procedures of a contemporary Islamic state must strictly follow the pattern evolved in the early period of Islam (an insistence for which there is not the slightest warrant in Qur'ān or Sunnah), these self-appointed "guardians" of Muḥammad's Message make it impossible for many educated Muslims to accept the *sharī'ah* as a practical proposition for the political exigencies of our time. By representing the idea of *jihād*, in clear contradiction to all Qur'ānic injunctions, as an instrument of aggressive expansion of Muslim rule over non-Muslim territories, they sow fear in the hearts of non-Muslims and fill many righteous Muslims with disgust at the thought of the injustice which such a tendency so obviously implies. And, finally, by claiming (again, without any warrant in Qur'ān or Sunnah) that the *sharī'ah* imposes on us the duty to discriminate, in all social aspects of life, between the Muslim and non-Muslim citizens of an Islamic state to the detriment of the non-Muslim minorities, they make it impossible for the minorities to bear with equanimity the thought that the country in which they live might become an Islamic state.

In order to overcome the apprehensions of the non-Muslim world in general and of our non-Muslim citizens in particular, we must be able to show that the sociopolitical scheme of Islam aims at justice for Muslim and non-Muslim alike, and that in our endeavor to set up a truly Islamic state we Muslims are moved by moral considerations alone. It is, in short, our duty to prove to the whole world that we really intend to live up to these words of the Qur'ān:

كنتم خير أمة أخرجت للناس تأمرون بالمعروف وتنهون عن المنكر وتؤمنون بالله

"You are the best community that has been sent forth to mankind [in that] you enjoin right and forbid wrong and have faith in God."[1] Our being a righteous community depends, therefore, on our being prepared to struggle, always and under all circumstances, for the upholding of justice and for the abolition of injustice for *all* people: and this should preclude the possibility of a truly Islamic community ever being unjust to the non-Muslims living in its midst.

The other difficulty before us—the one brought about by the sterile, formalistic views of the "conservative" Muslims regarding the nature and the methods of an Islamic state—can be surmounted only if we approach the problem of the political law laid down in Qur'ān and Sunnah in a creative spirit, independently of all "historical precedents" and all time-bound interpretations handed down from previous generations. In other words, we must be able to demonstrate, over the objections of our "conservatives," that the Law of Islam is not merely a subject for hair-splitting books of *fiqh* and wordy Friday sermons, but is a living, dynamic program

[1] Qur'ān 3:110.

of human life: a program sovereign in itself, entirely independent of any particular environment, and therefore practicable at all times and under all conditions: a program, in brief, that would not only not hamper our society's development but would, on the contrary, make it the most progressive, the most self-reliant, and the most vigorous of all existing societies.

The Need for a Code of Laws

I cannot conclude this discussion of the principles of the Islamic state without saying a few words about the need for a codification of Islamic Law.

We have seen that the foremost duty of an Islamic state consists in enforcing the ordinances of the *sharīʿah* in the territories under its jurisdiction[2]; and to this end we need a concise, clearly comprehensible code of *sharʿī* laws. But where is such a code to be found? The obvious answer is: In the *naṣṣ* ordinances of Qur'ān and Sunnah. But have these *naṣṣ* ordinances ever been brought out in their entirety and presented to the Muslim community without the deductive additions elaborated by conventional *fiqh?* The answer is, unfortunately, never. Instead of being given a true, simple—and therefore easily understandable—picture of Islamic Law, the Muslims are presented with a gigantic, many-sided edifice of *fiqhī* deductions and interpretations (a secondhand Islam, as it were) arrived at by individual scholars and schools of thought a thousand years ago. But these deductions and interpretations are not only many in number and most complicated: they frequently *contradict* one another in the most essential points of law. The views as to what Islam aims at and how a Muslim should behave in social and political matters are certainly not the same with, say, a Sunni *faqīh* of the Ḥanafī school, a "Twelver" Shīʿī, or a Ṣūfī —not to mention many lesser schools of thought. Which, then, of the various *fiqhī* systems should an Islamic state adopt as the basis of its code of public law?

One might, of course, argue that every Muslim country should

[2] See chapter iii, section on *Guiding Principles.*

utilize for this purpose the *fiqhī* teachings to which the majority of its population adheres: thus, in a country inhabited predominantly by Ḥanafīs, Ḥanafī *fiqh* should supply the basis of public law; in a predominantly Shī'ī country, Ja'farī *fiqh*; and so forth. But there are at least two weighty objections to such a procedure. On the one hand, none of the existing *fiqhī* systems truly corresponds to the needs of our time, being largely the outcome of deductions conditioned by the experiences of a time very much different from our own. And, on the other hand, it is inconceivable that in a state which claims to be Islamic, the *fiqhī* teachings acceptable only to one part of the population (even though that part be numerically preponderant) should be imposed on the minority within the community against its will, thus reducing it to the status of a minority in the political sense as well: for such an arbitrary procedure would flagrantly offend against the Qur'ānic principle of the brotherhood and equality of all Muslims. Consequently, an Islamic state must have at its disposal a code of the *sharī'ah* which (*a*) would be generally acceptable to all its Muslim citizens without distinction of the *fiqhī* schools to which they may belong, and (*b*) would bring out the eternal, unchangeable quality of the Divine Law in such a way as to demonstrate its applicability to all times and all stages of man's social and intellectual development.

That this twofold necessity is keenly felt in the modern world of Islam is evident, among other things, in the suggestions often made to the effect that the teachings of the existing *fiqhī* schools of thought should be harmonized among themselves and thereupon "revised in the light of modern thought and of modern conditions of life." It seems to me, however, that such an attempt would not only defeat its purpose but might even lead to most unfortunate developments as regards the attitude of the Muslims toward the problem of the *sharī'ah* as such.

First, a "harmonization" of the various schools of Islamic *fiqh*—however desirable on the surface—cannot possibly produce a code that would be simple and, therefore, accessible to a non-specialized Muslim of average intelligence, for it would amount to no more than an artificial coördination of the innumerable and highly speculative "deductions" of which the conventional *fiqh* (of all schools) is largely made up: and the result would be a still more complicated system of speculative *fiqh*.

Second, such a coördination would only perpetuate the confusion existing in the minds of many Muslims: a confusion between what has been ordained by God and His Apostle (in other words, what the Law-Giver has stipulated as law, in terms of law, in the *naṣṣ* of Qur'ān and Sunnah), on the one hand, and what generations of Muslim scholars have thought *about* the Law, on the other. Thus, our concept of the *sharī'ah* would again be chained to the ways of thought prevailing at a particular period of history—that is, to human, time-conditioned thought.

Third, an attempt to "revise" the *sharī'ah* in the light of modern conditions is bound to destroy the last vestige of permanency and stability which a Muslim instinctively—and correctly—associates with the concept of Divine Law. For if revision is necessary now, it will certainly again become necessary a few decades hence, when "modern conditions" will again have changed: and so on and on, until the Law of Islam will be entirely revised out of existence. If this were justified, what right would we have to claim that the Law-Giver has conceived the Law of Islam as an eternal proposition? Would it not, in that event, be much more appropriate to say that this Law, instead of *creating* conditions, is *subservient* to them—and that, therefore, it cannot be a Divine Law?

Our confusion cannot be resolved by such a defeatist attitude; it cannot and never will be resolved by our giving in on the point of the eternal validity and the unchangeable quality of the Divine Law. On the other hand, we cannot successfully maintain this validity and this quality unless we summon our courage to separate, with an utter disregard for all conventional attachments, God's true *sharī'ah* from all man-made, deductive, *fiqhī* laws. Briefly, the reduction of Islamic Law to its original scope and extent—the plain, self-evident (*ẓāhir*), unequivocal ordinances of Qur'ān and Sunnah—is the *only* way for the Muslims to regain a genuine understanding of Islam's ideology, to overcome their cultural stagnation and decay, to shed that pernicious automatism now so prevalent in religious thought, and to make the *sharī'ah* a living proposition for and in an Islamic state.

Method of Codification

For any Muslim community that is resolved to live according to the tenets of Islam and to translate its social and economic program into political action, the first step to be taken must be a codification of those *nuṣūṣ* of Qur'ān and Sunnah which contain self-evident laws relating to matters of public concern. In the context of an Islamic state, the procedure should be, I believe, somewhat along these lines:

(1) The *majlis ash-shūrā* shall elect a small panel of scholars representing the various schools of *fiqh*, fully conversant with the methodology and history of the Qur'ān and the science of *ḥadīth*, and entrust them with the codification. Under their terms of reference, they will have to concentrate exclusively on such ordinances of Qur'ān and Sunnah as (*a*) answer fully to the linguistic definition of *naṣṣ*—that is to say, injunctions and statements which are self-evident (*ẓāhir*) in their wording, having a particular meaning which does not admit more than one interpretation; (*b*) are expressed in terms of command (*amr*) or prohibition (*nahy*); and (*c*) have a direct bearing on man's social behavior and action.

(2) While a selection of *naṣṣ* ordinances from the Qur'ān is comparatively easy—because only one text is to be considered—the application of the above principles to *aḥādīth* will necessitate a thorough examination of each item against its proper historical background. Only Traditions which meet the highest standards of historical and technical criticism are to be considered, while Traditions which leave the slightest opening for legitimate objections regarding their authenticity should be excluded from the outset. (This, of course, does not mean that Traditions which are slightly defective from a purely technical point of view but otherwise bear all the marks of authenticity should not be utilized occasionally for

the purposes of *ijtihād*: what I wish to stress here is merely the inadmissibility of using such Traditions as material for the *shar'ī* code under discussion.) Particular care must be taken to differentiate between ordinances intended by the Prophet to be valid for all times and circumstances, and ordinances which were obviously meant to meet the needs of a particular occasion or time. This latter group of ordinances usually reveals itself as such in the very wording adopted by the Prophet, or in the accompanying explanatory remarks of the Companion responsible for the *ḥadīth* in question; and occasionally the time-bound quality of an injunction contained in one *ḥadīth* becomes evident through other *aḥādīth* relating to the same subject. Whenever no indication to the contrary is available, a *naṣṣ* ordinance emanating from a duly authenticated Tradition must be regarded as having universal validity.

(3) It is obvious that, in order to establish the *shar'ī* code, we must not confine ourselves to selecting disjointed verses of the Qur'ān or individual *aḥādīth*: in each and every instance, the entire context of Qur'ān and Sunnah must be taken fully into consideration. It sometimes happens that a Qur'ān verse which, by itself, does not seem to express a legal ordinance assumes the quality of a *naṣṣ* law as soon as it is read in conjunction with another verse or with an authentic *ḥadīth*. Still more frequently the same holds true for the Prophet's Sunnah. We should not forget that most of the existing *aḥādīth* give us no more than fragments of the Prophet's sayings or describe isolated incidents (often taken out of their historical context) in his life as leader and legislator: consequently, a legal ordinance ensuing from the Prophet may on occasion reveal itself as such only when we place several authentic *aḥādīth* side by side, or read the relevant *ḥadīth* in conjunction with a corresponding Qur'ān verse. In any event, one should never overlook the fact that Qur'ān and Sunnah form one integral whole, elucidating and amplifying one another: and so the proposed *shar'ī* code must contain cross references ranging over the whole context of both.

(4) The *naṣṣ* ordinances of Qur'ān and Sunnah thus established

should be placed together, arranged under specific headings relating to the various aspects of Muslim social and political life, and circulated among competent scholars throughout the Muslim world with a view to obtaining suggestions and criticism, especially with regard to the method by which ordinances based on *aḥādīth* have been treated. Stress should be laid on the fact that it is not intended to "reduce" Qur'ān and Sunnah to the extent of the *naṣṣ* ordinances contained in them: it should be made clear that this codification aims at no more than bringing out the ordinances which—by virtue of their *ẓāhir* quality—are not subject to conflicting interpretations and can, therefore, constitute the largest possible common denominator between the various *fiqhī* schools of thought. The fact that all statements in Qur'ān and Sunnah which may be interpreted in more than one way will *a priori* (under the original terms of reference issued to the codification committee) be excluded from the purview of the code will not only make the code acceptable to *all* Muslims, of whatever sect or *fiqhī* persuasion, but will also result in a code of public law that is small in volume, extremely concise, and therefore easily accessible to the understanding of every Muslim man and woman of average intelligence and education.

(5) The criticisms and suggestions received from the scholars among whom the proposed "minimum" code of *sharʿī* ordinances has been circulated shall be considered on their merits and utilized in the final revision of the collection, whereupon it shall be submitted to the *majlis ash-shūrā* for adoption as the Basic Law of the land.

Toward New Horizons

If we codify the social ordinances of the *sharīʿah* on the lines suggested above, the political ideology of Islam (taking the term "political" in its widest sense) will stand forth with a clarity which has hitherto been denied to it. Every one of its statutes will convey a precise meaning which admits of no conflicting interpretation; and every Muslim will know that, as a Muslim, he is bound to accept the unchallengeable authority of these *sharʿī* laws. The need for learned *ijtihād* will not thereby be abolished; it will be, if anything, intensified. We must remember that the true *sharīʿah* (consisting of the *naṣṣ* ordinances of Qurʾān and Sunnah) was never intended to cover every detail and every possible constellation of our lives, but is only a framework within which we are expected to unfold our creative powers and in the light of which we have to regulate our daily affairs. If we remember this, we realize at once how immense the field is within which we must exercise our independent reasoning. Naturally, there will always be differences between the various results of *ijtihādī* thinking. But what of it? Once the sociopolitical laws of the *sharīʿah* are established as the unchangeable basis of Muslim communal life, to all our differences of opinion on non-*sharʿī* matters will apply that immortal saying of the Prophet which I have already quoted elsewhere in this book:

إختلاف علماء أمتى رحمة

"The differences of opinion among the learned within my community are [a sign of] God's grace."

As things stand at present, nobody in his senses can claim to discern an evidence of "God's grace" in the dissensions and differences of opinion which have converted the modern world of Islam into a formless, chaotic, culturally unproductive mass of humanity. Lacking fundamental agreement as to what the sociopolitical Law of Islam really implies, these dissensions and differences of opinion do not increase our creative powers: rather they increase our doubts, our despondency, our cultural defeatism, and our disgust with ourselves and with our ideological heritage. And things are bound to go on in this way—which is leading to a gradual abandonment of Islam as a practical proposition and so to the ultimate dissolution of our culture—unless and until we rouse ourselves to the long-neglected task of codifying the sociopolitical laws of the *sharīʿah* and adopting them as a basis for our communal life. So long as this is left undone, the Muslims are bound to hold widely divergent—and therefore futile—views as to the social paths on which Islam expects us to progress: until, in the end, all our ideas of progress will be entirely divorced from Islam.

Do we Muslims wish this to happen? Or do we wish to make it clear—to ourselves no less than to the rest of the world—that Islam is a practical proposition for all times, and therefore for *our* time as well?

The ideology of Islam is as practicable or as impracticable as we Muslims choose to make it. It will remain impracticable if we continue to confine our concept of Islamic Law to the *fiqhī* concepts of our past; but its practicability will at once become apparent if we have the courage and imagination to approach it with fresh and unprejudiced minds, and exclude from its orbit all conventional, *fiqhī* "deductions." Obviously, such a reorientation of thought will be a painful process to many of us. It will imply a radical break with many habits of thought to which the Muslims have grown accustomed in the course of their history; the abandonment or modification of many social customs which have been "sanctified" by the usage of centuries; the renunciation of the complacent conviction that all the ways and byways of Muslim social life have been authoritatively and finally laid down in this or that book of *fiqh*: and all this will mean our moving forward toward horizons as yet uncharted. And because such a prospect is frightening to the more conservative among us, any endeavor directed toward this end will undoubtedly provoke a most lively resistance, especially from people who have made a kind of "vested interest" out of their unquestioning reliance on the views of the great *fuqahā*ʾ of our past, and a kind of virtue out of their own timidity in intellectual and social matters. But this opposition must not be allowed to deter us if we are conscious of desiring the triumph of Islam, and nothing but Islam.